PERMISSION TO ~~SCREW UP~~

SCREW UP

PERMISSION TO

~~SCREW UP~~

SCREW UP

How I Learned to Lead by Doing
(Almost) Everything Wrong

Kristen Hadeed

PORTFOLIO/PENGUIN

PORTFOLIO/PENGUIN
An imprint of Penguin Random House LLC
375 Hudson Street
New York, New York 10014

Copyright © 2017 by Kristen Hadeed

Most Portfolio books are available at a discount when purchased in quantity for sales promotions or corporate use. Special editions, which include personalized covers, excerpts, and corporate imprints, can be created when purchased in large quantities. For more information, please call (212) 572-2232 or e-mail specialmarkets@penguin randomhouse.com. Your local bookstore can also assist with discounted bulk purchases using the Penguin Random House corporate Business-to-Business program. For assistance in locating a participating retailer, e-mail B2B@penguinrandomhouse.com.

ISBN: 9781591848295 (hardcover)
ISBN: 9780698409385 (e-book)
ISBN: 9780525533290 (international edition)

Printed in the United States of America
10 9 8 7 6 5 4 3 2 1

Designed by Alissa Rose Theodor

Penguin is committed to publishing works of quality and integrity. In that spirit, we are proud to offer this book to our readers; however, the story, the experiences, and the words are the author's alone.

Some names and identifying characteristics have been changed to protect the privacy of the individuals involved.

To my sister, Lauren

My best friend, my rock, and my first business partner. Thanks for believing in me, for pushing me to stay true to who I am, and for always playing Ken so I could be Barbie. (Like you had a choice.)

CONTENTS

FOREWORD

Chin up. Smile. Stand up straight.

This is the language of ballet, an art form that is all about projecting perfection. And that is exactly what the audience sees. The perfect line. The perfect form. The perfect movement. You know . . . perfect. A look behind the scenes, however, reveals something quite different. The reality of ballet is anything but perfect, and creating the illusion that it is comes at a steep cost. Aching bodies. Mangled toes. Eating disorders and body dysmorphia. And any career success that ballerinas may achieve doesn't last long. Most retire in their thirties because of injuries and wear and tear on their bodies. Perfection, as it turns out, is a short-term strategy. The same is true in business.

So many leaders think perfection is the key to high-quality performance and high-quality service. And that can work, I guess, but not for long. Pushing people to be perfect all the time, as in ballet, comes at a cost. In business that cost is performance, innovation, and stability. Leaders who push for perfection burn out their people. They cause employees to work against one another rather than support one another. They create toxic environments where people are more likely to blame others than take responsibility themselves, where they hoard ideas instead of sharing them, and where they hold tight to best practices instead of passing them on to other members of the team, whom they view as competition. In cultures that demand perfection, employees and leaders alike mask gaps in training, cover up mistakes, and suppress feelings of doubt or concern. This is not a recipe to build a strong organization.

Unfortunately, perfection has become the modern standard. In our personal lives, we feel pressure to curate and filter our pictures so that our lives look "perfect" before we share them on social media. And organizations are just as susceptible as individuals. Many companies go to great lengths to present themselves as infallible too. Every decision is always the right decision until scandal or public outrage forces executives to admit their direction was anything but right. Consider Volkswagen falsifying emissions for its cars or United Airlines dragging a paying customer off its aircraft. It took tremendous public pressure before the leaders of these companies admitted they had made a mistake.

Perfect is an aspiration. An ideal. An unachievable goal. People who present themselves as perfect and maintain that all their work or all their decisions are perfect are totally untrustworthy. Be it in a sales call or a job interview, the person who says with confidence, "I am really good at *this*, but *that* is something I would want help with," is vastly more trustworthy and credible than someone who claims to be great at everything.

Perfection comes out of molds or off assembly lines. It is

not the natural state of things. And the great irony is that we value things made by hand more than we do things that come from machines, despite the fact that things from machines are more . . . perfect. Why, then, do so many leaders fail to recognize the same value when it comes to their people or, for that matter, themselves? Our foibles are what make us endearing. Our irregularities are what make us unique. Our human imperfections are what make us beautiful. This doesn't mean that we shouldn't strive to be better. But there is a huge difference between aspiring to be our best selves and claiming to be perfect. One is a journey of fulfillment. The other is a lie we tell ourselves and others. Good leaders know that their people will only truly thrive not when they are pushed to be perfect but when they are encouraged to be their natural best.

And this is exactly why Kristen Hadeed's work matters. As she built her business, Kristen learned more than the value of screwing up. She learned the value of imperfection. She learned how to create a culture in which her people feel safe being imperfect. And to feel safe being imperfect means feeling safe being vulnerable. That, in huge measure, is what has propelled her company's success and helped her people become some of the most innovative, productive, trustworthy, and cooperative employees out there.

I admit, "being vulnerable" sounds more like advice from a self-help book than a good way to conduct business or build a company. That is, until we understand what "vulnerable" looks like in a company. It doesn't mean we walk around crying all the time. "Vulnerable" in a corporate culture means that someone feels safe enough to raise their hand and say, "I don't feel qualified to do the job I've been asked to do. I need help." It means someone feels they can admit weakness or insecurity without fear of humiliation and the company can, in turn, offer additional training. It means someone feels they can walk into their boss's office and say, "I screwed up," without fear of putting their job, advancement, or reputation on the line. But for too many of us, vulnerable is exactly the thing we most certainly cannot be at work. Perfect (or the presentation of perfect) is our best option for security or advancement. Were it not for the fact that that's impossible, it could be a reasonably good strategy.

Creating a culture in which people feel safe to make mistakes, to reveal their weaknesses and imperfections, isn't easy, but it is what leadership is all about. Leadership is not about being in charge; it's about taking care of those in our charge and making people feel safe.

Permission to Screw Up is the story of what it means to be a leader. What is so astonishing about Kristen is how young she was when she figured it out. Kristen is not perfect. She is not a tech billionaire. Her company is not a unicorn. Her success is not the stuff of folklore and fantasy, which has unfortunately become the standard of success for so many in her generation. Her story is more human. More achievable. Less about winning a lottery and more about the work we need to do to inspire respect, loyalty, and remarkable teamwork. Her story is a far more trustworthy guide for how we should be building companies than too many of the other books we read on the same subject.

I was with Kristen at a leadership summit a few years ago. She was the youngest person there. Most of the others were seasoned titans of business who ran companies with revenues in the hundreds of millions and more. They were all good CEOs in the sense that they believed in a people-first approach to leadership. They all showed respect when their peers spoke. It was only when Kristen spoke, however, that everyone pulled out their notebooks. It was an amazing sight to see. The teachers became the students. Kristen is as humble as she is smart. She is aware of how much she still has to learn. And perhaps that's the reason we want to hear what she says: because with a supportive smile, she offers every one of us permission to screw up.

Simon Sinek
Author of *Start with Why* and *Leaders Eat Last*

PERMISSION TO

~~SCREW UP~~

SCREW UP

1 ~~SPEW~~ THE 45

It's a hundred-degree day in the middle of a scorching Florida summer.

I'm sitting in a comfy armchair, right smack in the middle of a beautifully decorated, air-conditioned apartment clubhouse where the residents congregate to play pool and watch football. I'm checking Facebook and texting my friends to make plans for the evening, and every few seconds, my eyes flick to the big clock on the wall in front of me.

It's been three hours, I think to myself. *Hope they're okay out there.*

Outside, sixty fellow college students, all of whom I hired within the last couple weeks, are scrubbing their way through hundreds of empty apartments, attempting to rid them of the filth left behind by the previous tenants—an incredibly tough job, especially when some of those tenants were frat guys (and roaches) who lived there for years without ever so much as lifting a toilet brush. Doubly tough when the AC units are down for maintenance and your novice boss doesn't even think to offer you a water break.

I contemplate checking on them but talk myself out of it. They had to have known what they were getting themselves into with a cleaning job. And anyway, they only have to do it for three weeks. Plus, I told them if they needed me, I'd be in the clubhouse.

I prop up my feet, put in my earbuds, and tell myself I have it all under control.

As you might have guessed, it doesn't take long for things to go south.

Like, way south.

—

Hours later, I'm still perched in my armchair, congratulating myself on how well the day is going so far. We're more than halfway through, and no one has run into a single problem yet (well, no one has *told* me about any problems, at least).

As I'm about to take the first bite of the Caesar salad I just had delivered, the clubhouse doors swing open, and my employees suddenly start shuffling through single file. It's not just a few of them: As I watch, fork halfway to my mouth, *forty-five* out of sixty of them crowd into the room.

For a split second, I think they're finished cleaning—which would be surprising, considering the amount of work I assigned them this morning—until I catch sight of their faces.

As they spot me, freshly showered, with my hair done and makeup meticulously applied, every single one of them scowls.

Yeesh. Why so serious?

"Hey, guys! How's it going?" I ask cheerfully, trying to lighten the mood.

Silence.

As they continue to make their way toward me, I can't help but cringe a little. They're all dripping in sweat. There are huge black grease marks on their arms and faces from scrubbing ovens and who knows what else, and they smell like a gross combo of body odor and moldy refrigerator.

"Bet you can't wait to shower!" I joke awkwardly, desperate for just *one* of them to crack a smile.

More silence.

What is going on?

Suddenly they start whispering to one another, and they begin nudging one person forward. I hear someone say something that sounds like "Do it."

Little do I know that I am about to experience the most humiliating thirty seconds of my life.

Slowly, one steps in front of the group. And then, carefully avoiding eye contact with me, she says, "We quit."

I almost drop my fork.

Wait . . . wh . . .

Before I can even think of a response, all forty-five of them turn around at exactly the same moment and begin to make their way out the big double glass doors, dragging their vacuums, buckets, and sponges with them.

Forty-five people quit.

At the *same time*.

Seventy-five percent of my team.

That's the moment that inspired my obsession with learning how to be a better leader.

—

I had no idea what I was in for when I started a cleaning company that hires only students while I was *still in college*. I—a millennial with hardly any leadership experience—decided I would hire other millennials—a notoriously tough group to work with and retain—to do backbreaking, dirty, physical labor that would include cleaning filthy toilets and scouring mildewy bathtubs. Somehow, I thought it would be easy. Ha.

It was anything but easy. I didn't know the first thing about building a business, let alone one that's part of an industry as unenticing as housecleaning. The day forty-five people walked out on me foreshadowed the many trials I'd face as a leader, which would only get more and more difficult. But with time, patience, and a lot of screwing up, I eventually learned how to overcome the challenges I had unwittingly taken on.

This is the true, imperfect story of how I went from that humiliating summer day to where I am now. It's about how I built a company where people want to be, and where millennials are loyal, productive, and empowered. Even as they do someone else's dirty work.

But before we get to all that, let's back up a bit. To the beginning.

I need to explain how I ended up in that clubhouse in the first place. You see, it was never even my intention to start a company.

—

In my sophomore year of college, I was studying finance at the University of Florida. Why finance? Well, I scoured Monster.com for the highest-paying jobs, and investment banking was at the top of the list. My dream was to move to Manhattan after graduation and get a job on Wall Street that paid a starting salary of no less than $100K per year.

At the moment, however, I was—as most college students are—broke. I had a scholarship, but it barely covered my expenses. This became a problem for me when I walked into the mall and fell in love with a pair of $99 jeans. (Designer jeans and living beyond my means: my nineteen-year-old self in a nutshell.)

I called my dad to see if he might be willing to help with my fashion emergency, even though I knew he'd say no. (If you saw what my dad wears every day, you'd understand that fashion is not exactly an emergency in his eyes.) He told me the one thing I didn't want to hear: Get a job.

Getting a job just to buy one pair of jeans sounded a bit extreme, and besides, college was my chance to live it up before I made it to the real world and had to work for the rest of my life. Scholarships had my basic needs covered. I didn't want a job with demanding, inflexible hours getting in the way of studying for midterms (or tailgating at football games), so I decided to figure out a way I could make the money quickly on my own.

This entrepreneurial way of thinking wasn't new to me: I've been a self-starter since I was six, when I started a babysitting service (even though I still needed a babysitter myself) and sold fake nails made of Elmer's glue to my first-grade classmates. After that came the Girls Club, a "friendship" club that members had to pay $5 to join. They also had to follow my thirteen rules (the seventh of which was simply "Obedience"). I signed the list, "Thanks, Your Leader, Kristen." Yeah. Definitely the same thing as friendship.

So when I found myself needing $99 in college, I wasn't in completely uncharted territory. Because Elmer's glue nails were no longer the hot commodity they were in elementary school, I went with the first viable enterprise that came to mind: cleaning. I figured it would be the best way to make enough money to buy my coveted denim in one go. I was willing to do whatever it took to get those jeans, even if it meant scrubbing a stranger's bathtub.

I put an ad on Craigslist to clean just one house. It went live on a Monday:

NEED HOUSECLEANING HELP? UNBEATABLE SERVICE AND PRICE

UF student will clean your entire house for $99 (plus tax). I've never been arrested, convicted of a crime, or anything else like that. I'm an extremely good student and have made the Dean's list each semester. I have a 3.8 GPA. Available immediately.

(I may have rounded up a bit on the GPA.)

By the end of the day, I had a potential customer: a busy

mom with a traveling husband, two dogs, two kids, and one messy four-thousand-square-foot house. She emailed me asking for a list of references and wanted to know if I supplied my own products.

References? Hmm.

I gave her the name and phone number of my aunt and my boyfriend at the time. I didn't tell her who they were—just that they were "previous clients" of mine. Luckily, she didn't call them.

Supply my own products? I think I can do that. . . .

I looked under my kitchen sink and found a bottle of glass cleaner and a sponge. I figured I could use my own toilet scrubber. (Gross.)

Yep, got everything I need.

She asked me the soonest date I had available, and we agreed on the following Wednesday afternoon. She gave me her address, and that was that.

The night before the big day, I went out to celebrate my friend's twenty-first birthday—which, predictably, meant I wasn't exactly feeling that great when I woke up. I slept through several alarms and desperately wished I could reschedule, but then I remembered the jeans. That's all it took to get me out of bed.

I pulled into the driveway just in time.

Wow, this place is huge!

I got out of my car, grabbed my small bag of cleaning supplies, and rang the doorbell.

"Hello!" she said as she cracked open the door, holding the collars of two horse-sized dogs as they tried to jump all over me. They were clearly dying to eat me alive. "Don't worry!" she said. "They're harmless! Come on in."

I stepped into her house. It felt like a sauna.

"Sorry it's so hot," she said. "Our AC unit is broken."

Faaaaantastic.

Head pounding and already breaking a sweat, I followed her to the kitchen as she locked the dogs behind a doggie gate that looked like it couldn't prevent a Chihuahua from escaping.

"You can put your cleaning supplies here," she instructed, pointing to the dining room. "I'm sure you have more to get out of your car, but I don't have a lot of time, so perhaps you can get them after I give you a tour?"

"Sure!" I said.

More supplies to get out of my car? Nope, this is it. Hope that isn't a problem.

"So here's the kitchen, and the big thing here, as you know, is using the right products on the glass stove top."

I didn't know.

As I followed her from room to room, I quickly learned there was a *lot* I didn't know about housecleaning.

Make all beds with hospital corners? Remove mildew in the master shower? What does mildew even look like?

She continued giving instructions as she gave me the tour, but I couldn't keep up. I knew this probably wouldn't end well.

"Okay, I think that's it!" she concluded. "Any questions?"

"I think I'm good!" I said in my fake-confident voice.

"Great. Well, I need to get back to the office. By the way,

how long do you think it will take? Just want to time it right with bringing the kids home."

Let's see. Four thousand square feet. Umm . . .

"Two hours?" Sounded reasonable to me.

"Wow! You're quick!" she exclaimed as she walked out the door. "Call me if you have any trouble!"

I decided to clean her daughter's bedroom first. By the time I'd removed the five million Barbies covering the floor and meticulously dusted three shelves of porcelain dolls, an hour had gone by.

I needed to pick up the pace. I went through the house, gathered all the laundry, and stuffed as much as I could into the washer. Then I moved on to the kitchen.

Special products for the glass stove top . . . like glass cleaner? Perfect. That's the one product I have with me. What are the odds?

Thirty minutes later, I realized my off-brand Windex was *not* cutting it; there were still grease spots everywhere. My two-hour time limit was up, and I had successfully straightened up one wing of the house and semicleaned the kitchen.

How was this taking so long? Even the dogs were judging me.

I decided to call her. I told her it would take another hour, and she was okay with that but warned me she would be coming home soon with the kids.

One hour later, she pulled into the driveway. I was still cleaning.

In the end, my two-hour estimate turned into more like

seven hours. I was still cleaning while she made her kids dinner, gave them baths, and put them to bed. But somehow, with a throbbing head, no AC, and only glass cleaner, a sponge, and a used toilet scrubber, I got through that entire house.

When I was done, it looked okay. Not great, but better than it did before. She paid me, and I left.

I thought that was the end of the story.

But really, it was just the beginning.

—

The next day, two hours after I left the mall triumphantly holding my new jeans, a funny thing happened. The woman who had hired me called again.

I was afraid she'd found the mildew I'd covered up with a shampoo bottle, so I let it go to voice mail. (How millennial of me.) But she wasn't calling to complain. Her message sounded something like this: "Hi, Kristen! Hope you're having a great day. Just wanted to touch base and see if we could set up a weekly schedule? I could really use the help."

It had never occurred to me that this could be more than a one-time thing. I decided I would love to have an extra $99 a week, so I started cleaning her house every Wednesday.

She was kind enough to let me use her products and teach me how she preferred things to be cleaned. I befriended the dogs and finally figured out the mystery of the glass stove top. (Use the clearly marked bottle of "glass stove top cleaner" under the kitchen sink.) Life was good.

Then she started telling her friends about me, and then they told their friends, who told *their* friends. As if that weren't crazy enough, I also forgot to take down the Craigslist ad. I woke up each morning to a few emails from people who wanted to hire me.

Some of these requests were a little weirder than others. One person asked me if I cleaned S&M playgrounds, and I said yes because I had no idea what those were. I showed up and quickly realized that I *did not* clean S&M playgrounds.

Another one emailed:

Hello Kristen,

What do you wear while cleaning? I'm not asking for sex, please don't get it wrong, but if you have some naughty clothes to wear while cleaning and are willing to wear those, we can discuss the details. You can come with one or two other friends if you want. Hope to hear from you soon.

I quickly declined. I didn't need another pair of jeans that badly.

Not all the inquiries were from creeps, though. I slowly started cleaning for more and more clients and found myself making pretty decent money. But it was physically exhausting: I cleaned before class, after class, even on the weekends.

I needed help.

I had a few friends who were broke, as I had been. I offered them jobs, but they refused. (Probably shouldn't have told them about the S&M guy.) So I decided to post an ad on Facebook. It read: "Fast cash, you pick your hours." From that I hired my first employee, Cacee.

Cacee was a sophomore at UF studying agricultural education and communication. She needed to make about $300 a month. Her reply to my ad ended with "I hope I'm what you are looking for! I'm a very dependable, responsible and clean person. Just looking for a job that can fit this hectic school schedule."

I told Cacee I would start her at minimum wage and give her raises as her performance got better, which was an idea I'd seen online somewhere.

Our first client together was memorable, to say the least. When we walked into the house, I thought I had stepped into a petting zoo. There were bunnies hopping around; a turtle was crossing the foyer; there were dogs barking, cats meowing, ducks waddling—and there was animal poop. Lots of poop. Everywhere.

There was also a baby crawling on the floor. A *human* baby.

The place smelled absolutely horrible. Black gunk, which we later figured out was tobacco, seeped from the walls. In the kitchen, I went to rest my hand on what appeared to be a dark countertop. As soon as my palm touched the surface, a billion fruit flies flew into the air, and I realized the counter was actually white. I looked at Cacee, and her face was starting to turn white too.

I motioned for her to come outside with me, as I told the client we needed to get more supplies out of the car.

We walked out the front door, coughing and gasping for

air. At the same time, we looked at each other and said, "Let's leave."

We got in the car and peeled out. I thought Cacee was going to quit, but amazingly, she didn't. Instead, she said we should call Child Protective Services. So I called. And then I called the client and told them I reported them.

I liked Cacee. She was fearless.

Business continued to grow after that, and Cacee started making well beyond her requested $300 paycheck. After just a couple months, we had eight regular clients, and we were cleaning houses together about five days per week. We eventually had to split up so we could take on more jobs as the requests kept coming in.

I ended up hiring a couple of other students to help Cacee and me. That's when it occurred to me that I didn't need to clean as much. Instead, I could handle all the incoming requests, schedule my employees to clean, and work on getting us more customers. Classes would be ending soon because summer was approaching, and my employees were about to have a lot of free time on their hands. They told me they wanted to use it to make more money. I certainly wasn't against that idea: I needed to save every penny I could for the Manhattan apartment of my dreams.

I created a flyer advertising our cleaning services, made some copies, and took them to different student apartment complexes around town. I figured if I put the advertisement in the leasing office, a resident might see it and call for a cleaning.

The first place I went to was a complex where a few of

my friends lived. I showed my flyers to Michael, the property manager. He agreed to hang up a couple, noting that my prices were surprisingly low. As I started to leave (intending to go home and make new flyers with higher prices), Michael said, "Hey, wait—I have an opportunity for you.

"In the summer, there's a three-week period when most students move out of their apartments, and all the units have to be cleaned before the new residents move in," he explained. "It's a very short time frame, and we have trouble finding cleaning companies that can handle all the work. You should hire a ton of people, and then I could pay your company to do it."

My lucky day.

"Email me, and we can set up a time to talk about a contract," he said.

I grabbed his business card, got in my car, rolled the windows down, and blasted music all the way home. *This is going to be the best summer ever*, I thought to myself.

Well, it was pretty great . . . for a little while.

—

As the glass doors closed on the last of my now-ex-employees, I sat alone in the clubhouse utterly dumbstruck. For a few minutes, I couldn't comprehend what had happened.

After the shock wore off, my mind started racing: Had I done something wrong? Had I not prepared them properly for the horrors of the job? Should I have checked on them?

My self-doubt soon escalated to anger. I started to pace around the room.

How dare they commit to working and then just drop everything and leave? I am paying them. I didn't have to give them this job. If they didn't want it, why did they even apply in the first place?

But my anger gave way to panic when the full magnitude of the problem hit me: My company was still contracted to clean *hundreds* of apartments, and so far, the team—all sixty of them—had done only a few dozen. I had just fifteen employees left to finish the work, and we had only a couple weeks before all the units had to be spotless. Period.

I started to cry, not knowing what the heck I was going to do. For a brief second, I thought about calling my parents for advice, but I didn't want to freak them out. I also thought about telling the client that I couldn't fulfill my end of the deal, but I didn't want to ruin my reputation.

That left me with two choices: I could go out and hire forty-five new people—which, in a city with thousands of students who needed summer jobs, would be possible but time-consuming—or I could go back to those forty-five people who quit and try to persuade them to give me another chance.

Plan B sounded faster, and I needed *fast*.

I left the clubhouse to go in search of the fifteen remaining people, who clearly hadn't gotten the "Let's all quit together" memo. I caught them just in time. Judging by the miserable looks on their faces when I found them, they weren't exactly loving the job either. I told them what happened with the rest of the team, and I must have come off as pretty desperate because they volunteered to drop everything and help me try to win the others back. (Or maybe it was that helping me sounded way better than cleaning.) We gathered in an empty apartment and quickly divided the forty-five names and phone numbers among us. We each found a surface to sit on—floors, countertops, windowsills—and called each person on the list *begging* them to come to an emergency meeting at my house that night. To get everyone to show up, I promised early paychecks for the work they'd done so far—and pizza. *Lots* of pizza.

Several hours later, the forty-five who had quit—and the fifteen who had helped me make the calls—were all cramming themselves into my small living room.

As I waited for them to get settled, I started pacing up and down the hallway, thinking about what I would say. I had concentrated so much on getting them here that I hadn't planned what I would do if they all actually showed up. Nothing in any of my business classes had prepared me for a situation like *this*. I was so nervous I was shaking.

I figured I should apologize, but I wasn't sure what to apologize *for*. In my eyes, I had done the things I thought bosses were supposed to do: I'd found work, hired people, and then stood by in case they needed me. But clearly, as evidenced by forty-five people essentially giving me the finger, I'd missed something.

Heart beating out of my chest, I walked out to face the roomful of sixty near strangers who, at the moment, weren't sure what to expect. I squeezed myself into the only free space left in the front of my living room, trying not to step on anyone. Then I closed my eyes, took a deep breath, and started talking.

"I'm sorry," I began, voice trembling a little.

They were barely making eye contact with me.

"It's my first time managing something as big as this, and . . . I'm not really sure what I'm doing."

A few started to look up. I took that as a sign to keep going.

"Actually, I have no clue what I'm doing. And I'm freaking out. These apartments have to get done, and I can't do it without your help. I need each and every one of you."

It was as if they could sense I was on the verge of a panic attack. They began putting away their cell phones and gave me their complete attention.

Come on, Kristen. Say something.

"I know cleaning can suck sometimes. Trust me, I've been in your shoes, and it's hard work."

A few chuckled, as if they didn't believe the freshly manicured boss from the clubhouse could bring herself to scrub a toilet.

"I promise you, I'm not afraid to get my hands dirty," I said, determined to convince them I was serious. "I'll prove it: I'll clean with you. We only have a couple weeks left and then it's over. We can do it together."

The room was quiet.

"Please give me another chance. Please."

Finally someone spoke up.

"All right, Kristen," came a voice from somewhere near

my couch. "I'll come back if you take care of the moldy re-frigerator in 208."

"Done," I said quickly. Small price to pay.

I noticed a few smiles around the room.

"How about that fan covered in black dust in 106?" an-other called out. "It'll rain dirt on you."

"Bring it on!" I cheered.

Whatever I was doing was working. The room was sud-denly filled with laughter as people began to shout out in-creasingly ridiculous assignments for me, including scrubbing an entire kitchen floor with a toothbrush. I accepted every one.

"So does this mean you guys are coming to work tomor-row?" I hollered over the noise. I didn't want to kill the mood, but I kinda needed to know.

"Why wait until tomorrow?!" someone hollered back. "Let's go tonight! Before she changes her mind!"

And that's exactly what we did: We left my house that night and went right back to the apartment complex where most of the team had walked out on me just hours earlier. Luckily they were kidding about most of their requests, but I kept my word that I would help them.

For the next couple weeks, I jumped into the trenches with my team. I went from apartment to apartment, getting sweaty and smelly as I helped them clean, giving them high fives (and bottled water). I got to work early each day so I could be there to greet them, and I was the last to leave at night, walk-ing each of them to their cars after they clocked out.

Most days we cleaned for eighteen hours straight. Not one person quit. And we finished our work early.

Early.

The managers of the apartment complex couldn't believe it. They were so impressed that they told me they'd already decided they wanted to hire us again next year. I ended up making a small profit, and my employees did pretty well themselves.

But what I was most proud of was winning back those forty-five people. In retrospect, I'm actually glad they walked out on me that summer. "The 45"—as I affectionately refer to them now—taught me one of the most important lessons I've ever learned: Leadership isn't sitting in an air-conditioned clubhouse with your feet propped up.

—

When the apartment contract came to an end, dozens of those I'd hired told me they wanted to keep working with me, and I realized that's what I wanted too: to continue with this crazy thing I'd started. I did it partially because I'd gotten a lot closer with the team during those last few weeks and I didn't have the heart to tell them they'd need to find other jobs.

But there was also something incredibly exciting about what I was doing. Running this business was far more interesting than anything I'd learned in my finance classes. I also suspected it was far more satisfying than a buy-as-many-jeans-as-you-want $100K investment-banker salary could ever be. So at the start of my senior year of college, I continued to look for cleaning work to keep us busy.

Luckily for me, I had no idea how hard building my company would be. Had I known what I was in for, there's no way I would've actually gone through with it. There's no class in business school called "Sh*t Is Going to Get Crazy 101."

If someone had told me when I started college that I would give up my dream of working on Wall Street after graduation to grow a cleaning business instead, I would have laughed my head off.

Now I laugh at myself for ever thinking I would have made a good investment banker.

—

My company has employed hundreds of students since I posted my first Craigslist ad in 2007.

When I tell people about what I do, the reaction I usually get is "How on earth do you get *millennials* to *clean*?" They act as if I've perfected a recipe for Gen Y Kool-Aid that they can't wait to get their hands on. National news outlets like Fox, PBS, and *Forbes* have published stories about my company because it's an anomaly: How can a business that requires hard, humbling, mundane work limit its hiring pool to a generation with a reputation for being entitled, lazy, and apathetic—and *survive*?

I get why people are so shocked by what I've managed to do and why they are so eager to know the secret. Millennials, born between 1982ish and 2004ish, are the largest generation in U.S. history and will make up 75 percent of the workforce by 2025. Business leaders especially are desperate to understand what makes millennials tick because millennials will determine the future success of their organizations.

As a millennial myself, I'm well versed in the stereotypes attached to my generation, which is often nicknamed "The Unemployables" and "Special Snowflakes." Rumor has it that we have no interest in paying our dues at the bottom and yet expect to rise straight to the top. People say we would rather send novel-length texts than subject ourselves to face-to-face conversation and that we are so thin-skinned when it comes to critical feedback that our supervisors walk on eggshells around us. They claim we refuse to stay in jobs where we don't feel like we are making an "impact" . . . despite the fact that we can't describe what making one would actually look like.

The stereotypes aren't entirely bogus. I've encountered plenty of students in my company who embody these descriptions to a T. But I've also met plenty of others who don't. The same goes for *every* generation: These days we occasionally hire seventeen- and eighteen-year-old high school students, who are referred to as Gen Z, and from time to time we've even employed baby boomers. (Who says you have to be young to be a student?) Like millennials, some of them fit their generational molds and some of them don't.

The point is that having a mostly millennial team has never been my biggest challenge in leading my company. What I know now that I didn't when I started this journey is that I basically chose the most difficult business model in the entire world.

First of all, we hire only students, which, regardless of whether they are millennials, comes with its own unique set of obstacles. A student workforce means that we have to accommodate class schedules, extracurriculars, internships, and a lot of "sudden illnesses" around spring break. It also means a mass exodus at the end of each semester: Our team members leave the company when they graduate from school.

Then there's the nature of the work we do. Seven days a week we have teams cleaning homes, offices, schools, condos, clinics, gyms, fraternity houses—you name it—at all hours of the day and sometimes into the night. Cleaning isn't particularly glamorous or fun; scrubbing and scouring someone else's mess can be downright disgusting, not to mention physically grueling. And forget about competitive pay: The average profit margin of a cleaning company is just 15 percent. We can barely afford to pay our students any more than minimum wage. They could easily earn larger paychecks making lattes or selling trendy clothes at a mall (both of which, I think, sound a lot more appealing). It's no surprise to me that the cleaning industry has an average turnover rate of 75 percent (meaning for every one hundred people hired, seventy-five quit).

As if that weren't enough, cleaning businesses tend to have low retention rates when it comes to clients too. The average company loses up to 55 percent of its customers annually because of poor-quality work. To have any chance of beating that statistic, companies need to make a significant investment in employee training...which they usually can't afford (15 percent profit margin, remember?).

I have no clue why anyone would consciously (or willingly) get into this business.

But this is the business that chose me.

Leading my company is an uphill battle. Most days I feel like I *still* haven't figured it all out, more than a decade later.

But this is what I do know.

People of all generations apply to work with us.

Our students love their jobs. Some love working with us so much that they have turned down higher-paying opportunities to stick around long term and help the company grow.

Our environment builds leaders: Many of our former team members leave with skills and confidence in themselves they didn't have when they came in, and they go off to start their own companies or are recruited for positions that by all accounts they shouldn't be ready for.

Our customers are happy because our people are happy. We don't even have to pay for advertising.

And it's all thanks to the extraordinary amount of screwing up I've done over the years.

I didn't learn how to create a place like this overnight. I didn't just run into a few hiccups and then experience runaway success. The moment The 45 walked out on me—and every other moment I failed as a leader after that—taught me something new, something that helped me make my company into what it is today. This book shares the hard-won leadership lessons I've learned since that day in the clubhouse. It's more about what I got wrong than what I got right. It's the story of the messes I made and how I cleaned them up.

This book is for anyone who wants to be a better leader, no matter your industry. No matter who you are or what your position is. No matter where you stand on the totem pole. No matter how young or how old you are. No matter how challenging your job is, no matter how badly your company culture sucks.

I hope my story will make you less afraid to screw up (a lot) by showing you that sometimes mistakes can be the best lessons. But most of all I hope it inspires you to keep going even on your toughest days. Even the days when you want to quit.

Even the days when forty-five people decide to quit on *you*.

2 ~~TIP SCRIP~~ SHEPHERD'S PIE

I woke up to my phone ringing at two A.M.

When I grabbed it off my nightstand, I saw a student's name on the screen.

Why is he calling me so late?

"Hello?" I answered quietly, trying not to wake up my roommates, who were sound asleep down the hall.

"Did I get a raise?" he asked.

Seriously. You are waking me up in the middle of the night to ask if you got a raise?

"What? No," I mumbled back, very groggy and slightly annoyed. "I mean, you're great and everything, but no, you did not get a raise. Why do you ask?"

"Ummm, well, normally, my paycheck is a couple hundred bucks," he said, "but right now I have a couple thousand in my account."

I was suddenly *wide* awake.

"WHAT?!" I screamed, practically jumping out of bed. My roommates were definitely up now.

I realized it was payday.

I told him I'd call him back and frantically searched for my laptop in the dark. The moment I found it, I snapped it open and banged on the keyboard with unnecessary force to try to get it to boot up faster. Seconds later (it felt like years), I logged onto our bank's website, hoping it was an easy fix.

No! No! NO!

The company's checking account balance was tens of thousands of dollars short of what it should've been.

How is this possib—? Oh no.

I suddenly realized the most likely explanation. Heart pounding, I entered my username and password into our payroll system so I could scan through the latest reports to confirm my suspicions—which proved to be correct. Lizzie, our HR intern, had made a huge mistake.

And I mean *huge*.

—

Lizzie was my first intern.

I met her when I was a guest speaker in her entrepreneurship class at the University of Florida, where I had been asked to share the story of how I started my business. After my presentation, she emailed me to ask if I offered unpaid internships that she could count toward school credit. *Why, yes*, I told her, *I do happen to offer those*. (Did she say free help? Music to a broke entrepreneur's ears.)

Lizzie was an exchange student from the UK, and she was looking to gain some solid HR experience during her year abroad in the States. The timing was perfect: I had graduated from college that spring, and I was putting everything I had into the company. That included $96.07 a month for a spot in a business incubator, our first official office space and a big step up from me working out of my living room. I couldn't afford to hire any office help on top of paying my rent, but *man*, did I need it. I'd take whatever Lizzie could offer.

It felt good to have an intern. At the incubator I shared common areas and workstations with entrepreneurs who were building companies just as I was, many of which had their own interns already. The day I walked in with Lizzie by my side it was like I finally belonged. (And I got major bonus points for her English accent.)

I spent several weeks training Lizzie on everything I knew about HR (which wasn't much): I handed over all the books I'd read, invited her to sit in on interviews with me, and even sent her to a few seminars so she could learn from experts in the field who were much more knowledgeable than I was. The first project I ever gave her was to create an employee handbook. When she turned in the final product, the opening line read: "This handbook is designed to inform you about a fairly boring topic—policies and procedures—and we will try to prevent you from falling asleep while reading it. We hope we will succeed!" I liked her style.

With every task I assigned her, Lizzie went above and beyond my expectations. I figured she could handle more. So one day I suggested she take on the biggest HR project yet: payroll. She looked at me wide-eyed: "You mean, for the *whole company*?"

I knew it was a huge responsibility. Every time I clicked "submit" on the payroll website, my palms got sweaty.

There was a lot of money behind that tiny click. And paying people is one of those things you just shouldn't screw up.

But I decided to let Lizzie take over anyway. Payroll took up several valuable hours of my week, time when I could be looking for more cleaning contracts instead. Plus, it was a great learning experience for her, and it would look stellar on her résumé. I taught Lizzie the ins and outs of the payroll software and did a few practice runs with her until she got the hang of it. Confident she was ready, I handed over the reins.

A few nights later, I was sitting in front of my laptop at two A.M. having heart palpitations.

—

As I sat on the floor of my bedroom, staring at the payroll reports in the dark, I spotted the error: Lizzie had mistakenly entered the total dollar amounts in the total hours column. Instead of paying people $200, for example, she'd paid them for two hundred *hours*. She'd accidentally overpaid twenty-seven students by a grand total of about $40,000.

$40K! I couldn't believe it. Our checking account didn't have room for a mistake that big. If each of those twenty-seven students actually spent the extra funds, we'd be broke. Super broke. Like *out-of-business* broke. I didn't know what to do (aside from check myself into a psychiatric center for the nervous breakdown I could feel coming on).

I called Lizzie. I needed her help fixing this ASAP.

"Hello? Kristen?" she answered, half asleep.

"I'm sorry to call you so late," I said, "but we have a big problem on our hands."

I thought *I* was having a panic attack, but Lizzie lost it. I could feel her anxiety through the phone. She immediately took full responsibility and started apologizing profusely. I calmed her down as best I could and told her we would get through it. I asked her if she had any ideas about what to do next.

After a few moments of thinking out loud, she had an answer.

"We could text all the students right now, tell them about the mix-up, and ask them not to spend the money before we reverse this," she suggested. It was a simple but solid plan.

Starting with the guy who woke me up at two A.M., Lizzie and I texted each of the twenty-seven students. (My thumbs still hurt when I think about how many times I typed "PLEASE DON'T SPEND IT!!" that night.) Then, together, we called our payroll rep. It was just after three A.M. by then, but miraculously she answered her cell phone. She told us there wasn't anything more we could do at the moment but promised to connect with Lizzie to figure out the next steps as soon as she got to the office that morning.

Texts and calls made, I couldn't go back to sleep, so I headed to the incubator at the first sign of daylight.

To my surprise, Lizzie was already there, sitting outside the door. I could tell she hadn't slept either.

She didn't wait for our payroll rep to get in touch with her. As soon as the clock hit nine A.M., Lizzie called the company for a status update. They told her they would reverse each transaction, but that it could take up to seven business days. Lizzie then decided to take the extra precaution of calling each of those twenty-seven students and explaining what happened, even though we had already texted them the night before.

After that, we waited.

And waited.

The days that followed were incredibly nerve-racking, to say the least. If we didn't get the money back, I wasn't sure if I'd have a business anymore. I had nightmares about our students buying scooters and fleeing Gainesville with their stacks of cash. I was pretty sure Lizzie was having the same bad dreams.

After a couple of extremely long days, we finally got the best news in the world: The payroll company had successfully reversed each of the transactions, and the overpaid money was back in our bank account. *Every single penny* of it. I could finally breathe again.

As soon as I got that phone call, I ran up to Lizzie, who was sitting at her desk, and gave her the biggest hug. We jumped up and down together, and I told her I was proud of how she handled the crisis. I could tell by the smile on her face that she was proud of herself too.

Two weeks later, when it was time to submit the next payroll, Lizzie asked if I wanted to do it instead.

"Why would I?" I replied. "You've got this."

She never made a payroll error again.

—

Though I wasn't aware of it at the time, the way I handled the payroll snafu with Lizzie would turn out to become a hallmark of my leadership credo: Trust people with enormous responsibilities, allow room for mess-ups, then give them the chance to fix their mistakes so they can learn from them.

This is not a philosophy I was taught in business school, and I didn't read about it in a leadership book. In fact, it wasn't a philosophy at all. It's just the way my dad taught me to approach things.

I've never doubted for a second that my dad loves me, but, man, there were times when I could have sworn he wanted to see me suffer. I can remember several times when I was really struggling with something—nothing serious, but to a kid, it sure seemed like it—and he refused to jump in and save the day. Once, in high school, I was completely stumped by my calculus homework. I didn't get the concept behind it at all, so I went to my dad and begged him to solve the problem for me. (He is really good at math.)

"I'm not just going to give you the answer," he said.

"Dad, *come on*," I pleaded. "If I don't get it right, it could bring down my grade in the class!"

He wasn't fazed.

"You've got to do this on your own, Kristen," he said. "If I solve it for you, how will you ever understand calculus? You'll thank me later. I promise."

(Yeah, right.)

He advised that I go back to my textbook and identify the specific areas where I was having trouble. Then he suggested I get to class early the next day and ask my teacher to review the material with me. It was the last thing I wanted to do, but I had no other choice. Turns out, sometimes father knows best: My teacher helped me grasp the concept I was struggling with and I learned how to solve the homework problem myself. By the end of the year I had one of the highest grades in the class.

There were plenty of other times while I was growing up that my dad took the "solve your own problems" approach—and eventually his methods wore off on my mom, who had always been a lot quicker to help my sister and me when we were younger.

As I got older, my problems grew with me. And my dad's tough-love approach only got tougher.

—

The day my parents found out about my company was also the day I leased my first car.

I was still in college, and I hadn't told them about my side gig yet. I knew my mom especially would think it was too much to juggle with school and would try to talk me out of it. And anyway, when I began cleaning houses, it was only a short-term thing. At the time, I still had my sights set on a future in the Big Apple.

While my dad was visiting me in Gainesville one weekend, we went to a car dealership so I could trade in the car I'd had since high school, which was having mechanical issues. He was certain I'd need a cosigner and I was certain I wouldn't, but there was only one way to find out. When the salesman brought me the lease application, I remember getting to the line that said:

Employer: _____

I wasn't sure what to do. My dad was sitting right there, and I knew it would cause a big to-do if I wrote down the real answer. I hadn't anticipated that *this* would be the moment he'd find out about my company. I thought about leaving it blank, but to get the car, I couldn't do that. And I *really* needed the car.

Here goes nothing.

"SELF-EMPLOYED," I proudly wrote in big, capital letters.

"STUDENT MAID BRIGADE," I wrote next to it in even larger, prouder letters.

Sure enough, the car salesman checked my credit, came back, and told me I was approved for a lease (at a high interest rate, but still).

My dad—who is an experienced attorney and therefore very good at interrogating people—couldn't get the questions out fast enough.

"What is Student Maid Brigade?"

"Wait, *how many* houses are you cleaning?"

"I'm sorry, did you say you have *employees*?"

"You've been doing this for *how* long?"

"You are incorporated, right? *Right?*"

"Kristen Kelly Hadeed, you better answer me *right now.*"

I drove away from the dealership with a new car that night, but I couldn't really enjoy it because my dad lectured me the entire way home—with my mom on speakerphone. His biggest concern (and rightfully so) was that I hadn't formally incorporated my business to protect against liability exposure (a phrase I vaguely remembered hearing in one of my business classes). My dad sent me an email later that night with the link to a website where I could register it, suggesting I get the ball rolling immediately. He ended his email with a piece of ominous, lawyerly wisdom: "One more thing. Before you incorporate, you might want to make sure you aren't infringing on anyone else's trademark. You know, copying the name of another company. Could result in major consequences."

I decided I didn't need to do that last part. What was the probability that someone else had named their business anything remotely close to Student Maid Brigade?

0 percent. I was sure of it.

So, a couple days later, I clicked the link in my dad's email, filled in my company name and my address, typed my dad's name as the registered agent, and paid something like $150 to the State of Florida. That's all it took to make Student Maid Brigade, Inc. officially official.

Not long afterward, I was hanging up flyers at apartment complexes around town when I met Michael, the manager who encouraged me to hire a small army of students to clean his apartments that summer. In order to make it happen, though, I'd need a lot more than a workforce. I'd also have to buy cleaning products, spray bottles, rags, sponges, vacuums, uniforms—all things I couldn't afford. I knew better than to ask my parents for a loan (if they didn't say yes to $99 jeans, they certainly weren't saying yes to this), so the only other option was getting a loan from a bank.

But the bankers were an even tougher sell than my parents. I was rejected many times for the same reasons:

"Aren't you still in school?"

"Why a *cleaning* company exactly?"

"You don't have enough experience."

"Where is your business plan?"

Experience? Business plan? For *real*? We're mopping floors, people, not inventing a prototype for NASA.

But if they wanted a business plan, I'd give them one. Just to make sure I did it right, I dug up a textbook from one of my classes that had a chapter on how to write one, and then showed my rough draft to Professor Rossi, my entrepreneurship instructor at UF. He gave me suggestions to improve my plan, and then, with his blessing, I went back to the bankers.

Even then, though, they turned me down, saying I didn't have enough collateral to secure a loan. It was discouraging, but I was determined to keep trying until someone eventually gave me some money.

And that's when I had an idea: I'd go back home and visit Pat—the bank officer who had opened my first account for me when I was sixteen—hoping our history would be reason enough for her to hear me out.

I was right. She was impressed with my business plan but even more impressed that I was willing to take on hundreds of vacated college apartments. She told me I had guts, and she agreed to give me a line of credit for $10,000. I had asked for five times that, but ten Gs was better than zero Gs, so I figured it was best to take it.

When I checked my bank account a couple days later and saw that $10,000 sitting there, I couldn't stop staring. My dad gave me another piece of vague wisdom—"I'd spend it wisely"—but I let that go in one ear and out the other. I had *ten thousand freaking dollars*. I couldn't even begin to think of how I could possibly spend it all. I was *rich*.

I'm absolutely mortified when I think of this now, but the first thing I did when the funds hit my account was call all my friends and request they bring a date and meet me at the best sushi restaurant in downtown Gainesville. That night I spent $1,000 of my $10,000 business loan on sushi and sake bombs.

My. *Business*. Loan.

I was definitely more responsible with the other $9,000. I spent it within a couple weeks, not on sushi or jeans but on cleaning chemicals, spray bottles, and business cards—all perfectly reasonable purchases. But I also bought car magnets, koozies, visors, coffee mugs, pens, and all kinds of other random promotional items that you *should not buy* when you're starting a company with only $9,000. In hindsight, when you have only $9,000, spending it wisely means hiring a CPA, getting an insurance policy, and maybe even saving some money so you can actually *pay* people. (Can you imagine telling someone, "Sorry I can't give you a paycheck, but here, want this cute coffee mug with our logo on it?")

With only a few weeks before the start of a busy summer, I had just two things left to do: meet with Michael to sign the apartment contract and hire more students to help with the work.

Days before the big meeting with Michael, I was sitting in my finance class, pretending to pay attention to interest rates and annuities while daydreaming about moving to New York the following year. I glanced down at my phone to look at the time and saw an email notification. There was a strict no-phone policy in class, but the millennial in me couldn't help checking it covertly under my desk.

Ms. Hadeed,

I represent Maid Brigade, Inc., which is the international franchisor of the Maid Brigade franchised home cleaning business. It has come to my attention that you are doing business as Student Maid Brigade, which is a clear violation of our federal trademark registrations on the name Maid Brigade. This is to demand that you immediately cease using Maid Brigade in your business name and in your business itself in any manner.

I felt my stomach drop.

How could this be possible? There had to be a mistake. In a frenzy, I grabbed my textbooks and told my professor I needed to go home. The moment I stepped outside, I called my dad and read the email to him.

Between sobs, I begged him to find out if I had really violated the law, thinking there might be some sort of loophole. I knew he was all about me solving my own problems, but I hoped that just this once, he'd forgo the teaching moment and help me. I wanted him to tell me he was going to call the attorney and get it all cleared up.

No such luck.

In response to my plea, I got silence, followed by "Well, I told you in my email to do your trademark research."

He then went on to tell me what would happen if I just ignored Maid Brigade's warning: I'd invite a federal trademark lawsuit with a potential loss of thousands of dollars that I didn't have. He explained the law in great detail to make sure I understood what I had done, but it was up to me, he said, to take it from here. And that meant contacting Maid Brigade's attorney *myself*. He told me I'd learn a lot more if I handled the situation on my own.

I was furious. I'm pretty sure I hung up on him. How could my father, an attorney—an expert when it came to this stuff—tell me I had to fix this *on my own*? An innocent mistake didn't deserve that response. I hadn't meant to do it. He would have called Maid Brigade's attorney if I were his client. Why wouldn't he go to bat for his own daughter?

I cried the whole way home from campus. After that, I spent two days trying to figure out how I'd respond to Maid Brigade's attorney. I finally sent him an email explaining that I was a student and that I couldn't afford the time or expense of throwing everything away and starting over, hoping he might tell me I wouldn't have to. He emailed back and told me (nicely) that I didn't have a choice. I had to cease using the name in public immediately and get rid of everything with our logo on it—which was practically everything

I had just purchased with the bulk of my loan. (Honestly, I was lucky he went so easy on me. Mr. Branch, if you are reading this, thank you.)

I went from being on top of the world to owing a bank $10,000, with only a couple vacuums and a few jugs of cleaning chemicals to show for it. I didn't even have a company name anymore. I was so mad at myself for spending $1,000 on sushi and sake; I really needed that money now. Lesson learned.

It was really hard to pick myself back up from that moment, but I had to do it. Summer was right around the corner and so was my biggest job yet. My pity party had to stop so I could focus on getting myself out of this mess I'd gotten into.

First I needed a new company name. I couldn't sign the contract with Michael without one. But try as I might, I couldn't come up with anything. Then, one hour before our meeting, while I was stopped at a traffic light, I had a breakthrough.

Kristen! You're an idiot. Just drop "Brigade" off the end!
Student Maid.

Perfect. And I wasn't infringing on anybody or anything— I checked. Twice.

—

I whipped into the parking lot of the apartment complex's corporate headquarters, ready to meet with Michael and put my John Hancock on the dotted line to seal the deal. I found my way to the conference room where we were supposed to meet, but when I got to the door, I stopped dead in my tracks. The room was *packed*. There were at least fifty people in there, maybe more. I thought it was supposed to be only Michael and me.

This can't be right. I must have the wrong place.

But then I spotted Michael, who was waving for me to come in.

It didn't take me long to find out that the fiftyish other people who were there were all cleaning business owners, and that I—contrary to my belief—did not yet have any contract. Turns out the company that owned the apartment complex Michael managed also owned dozens of other complexes in town. Most of the people in the room were there to *compete* for contracts to clean the various properties, including Michael's, during that upcoming summer. I would have understood that had I actually read the document he had given me months ago. Instead I'd gone out and gotten a loan for a contract that I *didn't even have*. I could already hear my dad's lecture.

Michael was one of about twenty property managers who stood at the front of the room. I watched as the other business owners went down the line, introducing themselves to each manager in an attempt to win the contract to clean their empty apartments. They were natural-born hustlers, and they all had business cards. I, on the other hand, was easily the youngest and least qualified person there. I didn't have a single business card to my name, thanks to having to throw them all away after my little trademark offense.

While everyone else made their sales pitches, I darted off

to hide in a corner. I clearly didn't belong there and every-one knew it. They didn't have to say it; I could just tell by the way they'd looked at me when I walked in. I wanted more than anything to find a secret doorway and disappear, but I couldn't. I had a big loan to pay back, and this was my only shot.

I took a deep breath and looked to the only source of strength available in that room: myself. I had to believe I could do this. I had to prove to these people they should hire my company. The banker who had finally approved my loan said I had guts. Well then, they had to be in there some-where.

You've got this, Kristen.

I stood up straight, walked toward the front, and hoped to goodness that I would remember my company name, considering I'd just changed it an hour before pulling into the parking lot.

"I know I'm young, but I can do this," I told the manag-ers, each handshake a little more confident (and less sweaty) than the one before it. "I hope you give me the chance to prove it to you."

Nine of them did.

—

A couple weeks later, I found myself sitting in that comfy armchair in the clubhouse, eating my Caesar salad, when out of nowhere, The 45 quit on me. As much as I wanted to call my parents for help, I didn't.

And now I understand that was my dad's plan all along.

For years he stood on the sidelines, giving me encouragement and guidance but leaving it up to me to solve my own
problems, even though it meant I'd make a ton of mistakes
(and boy, did I). He could have offered to verify the trademark before I incorporated. He could have helped me manage my business loan. He could have called Maid Brigade's
attorney for me. He could have done my calculus homework in high school. But he didn't do any of those things—
and not because he didn't care. In fact, it was the opposite.

My dad knew that if I was to be successful, he had to
push me to take responsibility. He supported me by giving
me a starting point—like warning me to do my research
and to spend my loan money wisely—but after that, it was
up to me. He wasn't abandoning me; he was sending me a
message: He trusted I was capable. And each time I over-
came a challenge or navigated a thorny situation by myself,
I internalized that message. The more I relied on my own
thinking and problem-solving skills, the stronger they
became—and the more confident I became. When The 45
walked out on me, I didn't pick up the phone to dial home
because I knew *I* could figure out a solution. I had done it
plenty of times before.

It took a long time to connect the dots, but I eventually
realized that if I wanted my business to survive, I'd have to
do the same thing for my team that my dad had done for me.

—

Not too long ago, I was asked to give a speech to a group
of CEOs about empowering millennials at work. (What did

I tell you about people thinking I have the recipe for Gen Y Kool-Aid?) I talked a lot about the do-it-yourself lessons my dad had taught me over the years and how they made me more independent. Afterward, I went to dinner with some of the executives, and as the meal was winding down, a woman approached me. She told me that my message had resonated with her, and she felt compelled to tell me a story about her daughter.

The previous summer her daughter had been home between semesters and needed extra money. She told her to go get a job, but when her daughter refused to take the initiative, the mother went out and found a position *for* her. Like . . . filled out the application. Even went so far as to write a script for her daughter's phone interview.

As she spoke, the woman's voice grew increasingly agitated. "All this time I was frustrated with my daughter," she said, "but now I'm upset with myself. I shouldn't have done the work for her. I thought I was helping."

She thanked me for shedding light on her own role in her daughter's problem and walked away.

Her story didn't surprise me. I have seen the same kind of thing happen in my own company on multiple occasions. Parents have called our office requesting a "status report" on their children's applications; they have asked me to give their kids a raise; they've filled out job applications for their kids right in front of me; they've called out sick for their children and asked for extra vacation days.

Student Maid isn't the only organization to experience the impact of overinvolved parents. According to a survey reported by CBS News and other media, four out of ten parents are involved in their child's job search, doing everything from sending résumés and cover letters on behalf of their children to attending the interview itself. I have no doubt that these so-called helicopter parents are acting from a place of love. They want their children to experience success. But reality—along with decades of research and countless articles—shows their efforts are backfiring. The result of all the hand-holding is a generation of people who are afraid to make their own decisions for fear they'll make the wrong ones, who have trouble functioning without guidance, and who struggle when it comes to thinking for themselves. When parents do everything for their children, they are inadvertently denying them the opportunity to develop trust in their own abilities and fulfill their leadership potential. Of course, not every millennial grew up with helicopter parents. But it isn't just the way we were raised that affects our ability to problem-solve; technology plays a part too. It's hard to make yourself stop and think when you've got access to Google 24-7.

All of this, I would soon learn, would make my role as a leader that much harder—and for a little while even drive me to do a bit of helicoptering myself.

—

Within a year of the infamous walkout of The 45, Student Maid was signing up new clients every day, and I was pouring every ounce of energy I had into the company: I scheduled every appointment, read every job application, conducted every interview, trained every team member, replied to every email, signed every contract, and answered every phone call. When someone would call and ask for the marketing department—or any specific department, for that matter—I would say, "Hang on just a moment while I transfer you," and then I would wait five seconds before saying in a different voice, "Hi there. How can I help you?" (Yeah, I know, it sounds like a bad sitcom.)

But clients weren't the only ones who kept my phone ringing constantly. Between their phone calls, I was fielding questions from our students left and right. They would call from cleaning jobsites to ask me whether they should mop the floor a second time if it still looked dirty (ya think?) or to ask what to do when the water from a faucet was too hot (turn the knob that says "cold," maybe?). One girl asked if she really had to clean a toilet (can't blame her for trying), and another wanted to know what to do when the client's front door was locked but the client was home (ever heard of knocking?). I don't know how many times someone called to tell me they'd accidentally set off an alarm or that they'd left behind a bottle of cleaning solution (or a broom, or a vacuum, or their entire bucket of supplies, or their *cleaning partner*) at a client's house and wanted to know what to do about it. My phone rang so much that I eventually became traumatized by the sound. (Seriously. To this day, if I ever hear my old ringtone, I promise you I will freak out.)

Getting these kinds of calls day in and day out made me feel like I had to spell out every step for our students just so they could get through a single day at work. I tried all kinds of quick fixes. I wrote long documents they could reference—the longest of which was sixty pages—that listed all the FAQs I could possibly think of; I gave them quizzes to test their knowledge after they read the documents, thinking that might limit the number of questions I'd get; and I even offered to pay them more if they could pass the test with a perfect score. But nothing seemed to work. Their first instinct was still to call me. It was as if many of our students couldn't solve their own problems or make decisions without deferring to someone else, and unless I made myself available to guide them, they'd be paralyzed by indecision and end up doing nothing. It was killing me (and my phone battery). "Exhausted" is an understatement.

Lizzie was a huge help, but there was only so much she could do, and I knew she would be returning to England soon. I desperately needed someone more permanent, not just to handle HR but to take over other aspects of the business. It couldn't be just anyone, though. I'd be trusting them to manage the day-to-day operations of Student Maid so I could focus on getting more clients and growing it into the biggest and best cleaning company in the world (okay, maybe just in Gainesville). Luckily, I didn't have to look very far. I already had the ideal person in mind.

Abby had been cleaning houses with us for about a year. I had hired her in my living room when she was a junior in college, and she had quickly become Student Maid's rising star. She was smart, proactive, hardworking, and honest, and she had a natural ownership mentality. I trusted her with every bone in my body, and I couldn't imagine finding anyone better to help me build Student Maid. So I worked like a dog until I could offer her a small full-time salary.

But my dreams were crushed when, as I feared, she didn't drop everything and say yes to my job offer. Abby had been interning at a large hotel chain in addition to cleaning at Student Maid, and they'd offered her a full-time position as well. She wasn't sure what she wanted to do with her life after college, and she needed time to think about it. She told me to keep looking so she didn't hold me up while she figured it out. After a few disappointing weeks of waiting around for her anyway, I knew I had to move on. But there was no one else in my company anywhere close to graduating.

And that's when Erin entered the scene.

Erin and I knew each other growing up and were friends throughout high school. When I learned from one of our former teachers that Erin wasn't happy in her job and had relocated back to Florida, I immediately got in touch with her.

Erin didn't have the cleaning knowledge that Abby had, but from what I remembered about her, she was never late for anything, and she was extremely thorough and detail oriented. I called Erin to offer her the position and emailed her exactly the same offer I had just pitched to Abby. She accepted and moved to Gainesville a few weeks later.

Soon after we decided on Erin's start date, I got a phone call from Abby. She was so excited to tell me: She had decided to turn down the job at the hotel and she was at last accepting my offer. (And *that* is what you call getting yourself into a pickle.)

Even though I really wanted to give the position to Abby, I had already promised it to Erin. I couldn't afford to pay them both a salary, but I knew I couldn't let Abby get away. If she had turned down a fancy job offer elsewhere for Student Maid, it meant she had just as much faith in me as I had in her. I told her I could offer her only $9 per hour and lots of hugs until we had more money.

To my astonishment, she said, "Count me in."

So just like that, there were three of us. (I would have said four, but Lizzie was on a plane back to the UK by the end of Erin and Abby's first week.)

Because Erin hadn't cleaned houses as Abby had, I asked her to spend a few days scrubbing toilets alongside our students so she could get a feel for what they went through (and show them that she wasn't afraid of a little grime). After that, I wasn't sure where to start. There was so much that Erin and Abby would need to learn about the business. I explained the basics of the company to them: what to say to clients on the phone, how to book appointments, how our invoicing system worked, how to order supplies, what to do when someone requests that we clean their S&M playground, how to not overpay twenty-seven people, etc. I arranged for them to shadow me for a few days so they could get a feel for the tasks they'd have to take over, and I gave them plenty of opportunities to ask questions.

After that, I made them lists. Very long, very detailed lists that told them exactly what to do and how to do it. Kind of like the sixty-page document I made for the students, except I emailed these to Erin and Abby *every single morning.*

TO: Erin

SUBJECT: Updated to-do list

Accomplish as much as you can today:

· Check on cleaning supplies. I have a feeling we are low. If we are, refill them.

· Get red vacuum fixed if it needs to be fixed.

· For services on Christmas, we technically can charge a surcharge. We did that last year. I think we should, maybe an extra $40. What do you think? Let's do $40.

· Email students who have not given us their spring semester schedule yet. I sent you their names and email addresses in a separate email, as well as exactly what to say to them.

This is just the first part of a *super long* email.

As with the students, these lists didn't help quite as much as I hoped they would. Even with Erin and Abby in charge of the daily operations full time, my job was just as hard. I was still the person who had to answer every question and handle every catastrophe. It didn't matter what I was doing—making a quick run to the grocery store, grabbing a bite to eat, sleeping—I always had to have my cell phone nearby (fully charged). *Everywhere* I went I pulled around an obnoxious briefcase on wheels that housed my laptop, along with extra batteries and chargers and all the important documents I might need to reference in the event of a crisis. (I quickly earned the nickname "Hot Wheels.") If I ever wanted to go out of town overnight, *fuhgettaboutit*. I restricted myself to places that were a short drive from Gainesville, just in case something went wrong and I needed to get back quickly.

By this point, it had been about two years since I graduated from college and I still hadn't taken a *real* vacation. Being in constant work mode had become my new normal; I had forgotten what it felt like to take some time for myself. I finally hit a breaking point and told Erin and Abby I needed to get away, and thankfully, they agreed to hold down the fort.

But this time I wasn't driving. This time I'd be boarding a *plane* and flying to St. Louis, where I'd spend a relaxing weekend *all by myself*. (I was still bringing my phone and wheels, of course. I couldn't get too crazy.)

Before I left, I made the list of all lists for Erin and Abby. I thought of every potential situation that might occur while I was gone and spelled out exactly how to handle each one. Many of the scenarios I came up with were less likely to happen than all three of us getting struck by lightning at the same time (while also being attacked by sharks), but at least all my bases were covered. I told all our students to call Erin and Abby—*not* me—if they needed anything. I felt like I had done everything I could to prepare the team for three days and two nights without me.

I could practically taste the room service I would soon be ordering from my hotel bed.

—

As I crammed my suitcases into my car, I couldn't help but smile. I'd packed three huge, overweight bags for what was only a three-day trip, but I didn't care. I was in vacation mode. I got in my car and rolled the windows down, waving to each jogger and dog walker I passed as I made my way to Gainesville's tiny airport.

By ten A.M. I was all checked in and sitting at my gate. I stared at my phone while I waited for my zone to be announced.

No missed calls, no texts, no emails. Nothing.

I didn't know what to do with myself. I took a deep, relaxing breath as I thought about all the sleeping in I'd be doing over the next three days.

And then—midbreath—the gravity of the situation hit me like a bucket of cold, soapy mop water: This would be the first time I was leaving Student Maid in someone else's care for an extended period of time . . . and I wouldn't be able to get back in an hour or two if there was a problem.

It's gonna be fine, I told myself. *You hear me? Fine.* But the thoughts stayed with me as I boarded the plane. By the time we touched down in Atlanta for my layover, I was kind of freaking out.

I turned my phone back on.

No texts. No voice mails.

I opened my email, holding my phone at arm's length and wincing as I waited for the app to load. Something bad was *definitely* going to be in there. I was sure of it.

But still . . . nothing. I refreshed it five times in a row just to be sure. I couldn't help but think about the silence in the clubhouse right before The 45 staged their mass walkout.

Kristen, you're being ridiculous. Maybe no news really is good news this time. Go get a beer and chill.

I decided to take my own advice and wandered over to the airport bar, where I sipped a Blue Moon and continued to talk myself down from the ledge I was on. By the time I got to my gate, I was feeling better, my worries replaced by visions of myself relaxing on my hotel balcony.

Just as I was shoving my briefcase into the overhead compartment, I felt my phone vibrate in my back pocket.

Damn it.

I pulled it out and saw a text from Abby.

"SHEPHERD'S PIE. CALL ASAP!!"

Oh no. No no no no no no. This cannot be happening. Please tell me this isn't happening!

To the rest of the world, shepherd's pie is a traditional English dish of meat and potatoes. But to Erin, Abby, and me, "shepherd's pie" was a code that meant something was going horribly wrong at Student Maid. (How did we choose that phrase in particular? No clue.) The rules were very simple: If I ever got a text from one of them containing the words "shepherd's pie," I had to drop everything, no matter where I was or what I was doing, and call them.

I thought about the other times Erin and Abby had used the code in the past: They'd used it once when a bin of microfiber rags caught fire spontaneously (never knew *that* could happen) and again when a client was so upset we'd spilled bleach on her designer rug that she threatened to sue us. Each time, I had come to the rescue and put out the fire (sometimes literally).

I need to get off this plane, I thought. *Right now.*

My phone vibrated again. This time Erin was calling me. I knew whatever was going on back at the office had to be *bad*. What could it be that I hadn't covered in my massive list?

As I was about to answer Erin's call, the flight attendant walked over and sternly told me to put my phone in airplane mode, then lingered nearby to make sure I did.

There was nothing I could do. I turned the phone off, tightened my seatbelt, and grabbed the barf bag.

—

By the time the plane started its descent into St. Louis, I was absolutely certain Student Maid was in ruins.

But as I turned on my phone and scrolled through the many texts from Erin and Abby, an amazing thing happened: The tone of the texts changed. They went from screaming, "SHEPHERD'S PIE" and "NEED YOU NOW" to "Everything is OK," "We figured it out," and even a ":-)."

Turns out a student had slipped and fallen in a client's garage. Even though she was a little banged up, she didn't want to go to the clinic and get medical treatment through our workers' comp coverage. She insisted she was okay, but Erin and Abby weren't convinced. I had briefed them on what to do if someone got hurt on the job, of course, but never taught them what to do if someone refused to get help after getting injured.

Once they realized I wasn't calling them back, they got in touch with our insurance company to go over what they needed to do legally to ensure they didn't make the situation any worse. Then they explained every option available to the student as thoroughly as possible until they were sure she was completely okay with her choice to refuse treatment. They got her refusal in writing and sent off the necessary paperwork to the workers' comp people, and that was it.

They didn't need me.

At all.

I wouldn't even have known what to do in that situation.

For the first time since they'd started at Student Maid, Erin and Abby had no choice but to rely on themselves and their own thinking. So they did. Very capably, I might add. They had all the smarts they needed to find the answers. They always had; it's why I hired them in the first place. The missing piece was opportunity. I was the one who had been getting in their way. Up until that point, when things got tough, all they had to do was say a code word and I'd hop in my helicopter and zoom right over.

When Erin and Abby told me the story of how they'd solved their own "shepherd's pie" dilemma, I could feel their pride through the phone. I realized they were proud because *they* had found the solution and got to take credit for it instead of acting on my orders. It's what I felt when I finally solved my calculus assignment on my own in high school, and what Lizzie felt after her plan worked to fix the payroll disaster.

When I returned from my St. Louis trip, I reminded myself to step back and let Erin and Abby step up more often. I did away with the detailed to-do lists and made it their responsibility to figure things out and handle predicaments as they arose. The more I got out of their way, the more independent and confident they both became. They called me less and less, and I finally felt like I didn't have to carry everything on my shoulders (or in my briefcase). I don't remember getting another "shepherd's pie" message after that.

Seeing how much Erin and Abby had grown made me want *everyone* at Student Maid to experience that kind of self-reliance and the satisfaction that came along with it. And that meant no more protecting anyone from making mistakes. It meant keeping my helicopter grounded.

It became my mission to make Student Maid a place where people had room to screw up and to figure things out on their own without having to worry about losing their jobs in the process. I figured that if I succeeded, it would be a win for all of us: Our students would gain problem-solving skills that would help them thrive not only in their jobs at Student Maid but also in their future pursuits; they would learn to trust themselves and become more independent; and they'd be able to take pride in their accomplishments. Even when they messed up, they'd learn something from it. Heck, if Lizzie could bounce back from a $40K mistake, I knew they all could bounce back from whatever screwups they made. In the end, I'd get a stronger, more reliable team (and *much* more relaxing vacations).

I guess that's when I started channeling my father. I

began to make myself less available to our students and no longer kept my phone glued to my hand. If someone called while I was in a meeting, I refrained from stepping out to answer. I'd let it go to voice mail instead, and sometimes, when I wasn't busy, I'd let it go to voice mail anyway. Often the person would have the problem figured out by the time I called them back. I didn't ignore *every* call, of course—I worried that would send the message that I didn't care about my team—but it was very different from my old approach of picking up on the first ring and dropping everything to come to the rescue.

Sometimes they really needed my help. If they'd called a few times in a row or walked into my office and asked me for my advice, I gave them my attention as soon as I could. But I took a different route: Instead of solving their problem for them, I asked them what *they* thought the solution should be. And unless their idea would burn the place down or kill someone, I told them to roll with it. If they *didn't* have any ideas, I told them to think about it and get back to me when they had two potential solutions. Then I'd tell them, "Either one sounds good to me." Sometimes they handled situations the way I would have. Other times they handled them better. Of course, every now and again their ideas were questionable. But even in those circumstances, I'd bite my tongue because I knew they'd learn from the outcome and handle it differently the next time around.

Soon the whole company was operating with a new attitude.

Training new recruits became more about teaching them

how to solve problems than about teaching them how to clean. In the past I'd held training sessions at my house (genius, I know; my house was always spotless), and I would "stage" them by hiding a piece of trash under the couch to see if the trainees found it or by leaving things in the dryer to see if they would think to open it and fold whatever was inside. It wasn't until they passed this test several times that they could actually set foot in a *real* client's home. Eventually I realized that throwing people into real-life situations headfirst was more effective (even if it meant I'd have to go back to making my own bed).

I got rid of those practice scenarios. Instead we did a quick overview of our products and techniques and then scheduled trainees to clean a real client's house with a team member who had some experience. Each team got a copy of our cleaning checklist—a list of all the things our website promised we'd do in someone's home—in addition to the client's specific requests, and we told our students we expected them to adhere to both while meeting our high quality standards. But *how* they chose to accomplish that was now up to them. Obviously, the more experienced student could remind the newbies which product to use or show them a technique if they asked, but if something unexpected popped up, we instructed the veteran not to fix it for them or tell them how to handle it. Instead they should support the trainee in finding their own solution.

Besides being more cost-effective, training this way had other benefits. Students were becoming empowered to make decisions without consulting Erin, Abby, or me. When one team realized they'd cleaned a client's neighbor's house by mistake (yes, this really happened), they took ownership and explained the mix-up without asking Erin or Abby to handle it for them. Another time a team member decided to send home a sick partner and finish up the job himself instead of asking for guidance. And when one team noticed a pipe had burst in a client's bathroom, they immediately called the client and prevented the house from flooding instead of contacting our office in a panic. Our hands-off approach was doing exactly what it was intended to do.

Nowadays we give our students even more autonomy than we did back then. We used to have experienced team members inspect more than 75 percent of our jobs for quality each day, but now we hardly inspect any at all (unless a client specifically requests it). In the past we never shared pricing information with our students. They had to text us when they arrived at a client's home and then notify us when they were done so we could tell them how much to charge the customer. We feared they might calculate it incorrectly. Now we give them the pricing formula and it's up to them to figure it out. The message we're sending our students every time we ask them to do something on their own is "I trust you, and I believe you are capable."

The shepherd's-pie-on-the-plane incident helped me understand my role as a leader better. It was my responsibility to guide and support the Student Maid team—not to direct their actions, make their decisions, and solve their problems for them. It was my job to provide them with opportunities where they could develop grit, self-reliance, and self-confidence—just as Erin, Abby, and Lizzie did when I gave them the chance.

Just as I did when my dad gave me the chance.

—

When we make people feel confident in themselves and in their decisions at work, they don't want to go anywhere else.

I know this because of stories like Monique's.

Monique joined our team one busy summer. I was at an apartment complex assigning units to our students, and she just so happened to be standing nearby when I realized that all the apartments we had to clean that day were locked. The manager of the property was very strict about the keys: She gave me one ring with more than a hundred keys on it and told me we weren't allowed to split them up and hand them out. She also said if we lost the ring, each key would cost us $50 to replace. There were about seventy students waiting on me for their cleaning assignments, and I didn't want to just leave them standing there while I went to unlock all the doors, so I turned to the person standing closest to me and asked for her help. It was Monique. Even though it was only her second or third day on the job and I'd just met her, I handed her the list of apartments and told her how much it'd cost us if she lost the keys, and off she went to unlock doors. She later returned the key ring completely intact and I thanked her, but I never knew just how impactful that day would be for the two of us.

Monique ended up staying on our team while she worked to earn a degree in interior design, and years later she actually turned down a job at a prestigious firm for a career with Student Maid. It was the lack of trust she'd felt at the design firm that influenced her decision most. When she interned there, she wasn't allowed to attend company meetings, she couldn't work on her own projects, and the biggest assignment she got was moving an outlet up an inch and a half on a drawing. When Monique shares the story of how she ended up at Student Maid, she tells people it all started with the day I handed her that key ring. She says it felt good to be trusted with something so significant, especially during her first week on the job. Today Monique is an indispensable leader in our company. She teaches others to be leaders, and she encourages them to hand over the keys to the people beside them too.

I also know it's working because of stories like Lizzie's.

Years after the infamous $40K error, Lizzie has a successful career in the UK. Not long ago, she came back to the States for vacation and stopped in Gainesville to have breakfast with me. That's when she told me how much her internship at Student Maid had shaped her future: Not only did the payroll disaster become her go-to story in every job interview she had, but sharing how she got through it became the reason companies wanted to hire her. She also said that my choice to trust her again with payroll, even after she messed up, is the reason she now tries to be the same kind of leader for the people on her team.

We can't just throw people in and expect they'll succeed.

There has to be a balance. First, people need to be aware of what's expected of them. We need to communicate the responsibility that comes along with what we are asking of them, like when Monique knew that each key would cost $50 to replace if she lost the ring. We expect they will solve their own challenges when they arise, but it doesn't mean we don't support them. When Lizzie made the payroll mistake, I wasn't MIA. I acted as her sounding board and stood by her the entire time. But she was the one who came up with the plan. I just followed her lead.

Not everyone thrives in our environment. Some have a harder time with it than others. Sometimes people have to leave because they can't handle it. Sometimes the mistakes are so huge and our people so overwhelmed that we step in to save them from catastrophe. No teaching moment is worth sacrificing someone's well-being.

Then you've got the people who keep messing up and aren't learning from their mistakes. How many missteps is too many? Where do you draw the line? These are all tough questions that, as you'll see later on, I've wrestled with myself.

And finally, what is the balance between letting someone struggle to solve a problem and knowing when to jump in and solve it for them? You have to figure out how high your screwup tolerance is. Thanks to Lizzie, mine started pretty high. But it doesn't require trusting someone to solve a $40K mistake to empower them or earn their loyalty. Sometimes it's the smallest acts—like handing someone a ring of keys—that have the biggest impact and define a person's entire outlook on a company . . . and themselves.

—

It's only now, after I've watched our students struggle just as my dad watched me struggle, that I understand how much courage it takes to stay on the sidelines. When we care about people, we want to jump in and help them. But if we do, they'll never grow.

The next time you see someone struggling, remind yourself that they don't need you to save them. They don't need the answer to their problem. They need to know they are capable of solving it themselves. That they can be their own superhero. If they can take responsibility and get through the hard stuff on their own, they will be so much better off.

I know I am.

3 ~~SUBTANS~~ BEHIND THE SCREENS

That's it. This is the last straw.

I stormed into my office and slammed the door shut. I paced around the room, trying to let off some steam.

What was she thinking? How could she be so stupid?

Courtney—one of our students—had struck again. Apparently, she had interpreted my new self-management philosophy of "Make your own decisions" to mean "It's a freaking free-for-all." Within the last couple weeks, her cleaning partners had spotted her spraying on a client's perfume, trying on a client's high heels, and calling her friends from a client's landline.

As if all that weren't enough to drive me crazy, I had just been informed of Courtney's latest escapade: playing "Mary Had a Little Lamb" on a very expensive, very off-limits antique piano in the middle of a client's living room. The living room she was supposed to be vacuuming. Unreal.

I hadn't talked to Courtney about any of her offenses yet—I was waiting for the perfect moment—but today was the day. Any minute now, she'd be stopping by the office to refill her supplies before heading out to clean, and I was going to give her a serious (and I mean *serious!*) talking-to.

I kept running the play-by-play in my head: As soon as I heard her sweet but oh-so-misleading voice, I would leave my desk, walk straight up to her, and tell her we needed to talk . . . alone. After that, I'd look her in the eye—calm, cool, and collected—and tell her if she ever did anything to jeopardize Student Maid's reputation again, she'd be done for good. I'd finish it off with an intense stare down until she apologized profusely and begged me to go easy on her. Maybe I would . . . *or maybe I wouldn't.*

Mid-daydream, I heard our front door swing open.

Courtney.

I poked my head into the hallway and sure enough, there she was, topping off her glass cleaner and saying, "Morning, y'all!" as if she were the most innocent person in the world.

Time to show her who's boss.

I started walking toward her.

You aren't getting away with it this time.

She looked up. We made eye contact.

Oh God.

She smiled and reached out for a hug.

"Courtney! Hi!" I blurted, arms wide open, leaning in for the biggest hug I'd quite possibly ever given anyone in my life. "How *are* you? How's school? Can I help you carry these supplies out to your car?"

Five minutes later I was standing in the parking lot, waving and smiling at Courtney as she started her engine. "I know you'll do a great job today!" I shouted as she drove away. "Make us proud!"

. . . Okay.

So.

Things didn't go *exactly* as I had envisioned they would.

There was no way I was actually going to confront Courtney. That level of badassery existed only in my head. I had never confronted anyone in my company before. Ever. I just wasn't that kind of leader.

I preferred to be the kind who stood on the sidelines with pom-poms instead: a *cheer*leader.

—

I remember the first time my words lifted a person's spirits at Student Maid.

It happened during the summer of The 45, soon after I'd won back my team. I was making my rounds to each apartment, delivering water bottles and thanking the students for working so hard. As I walked into one of the units, I saw only two students cleaning, but according to my notes, there should have been three.

"Hey, guys!" I said, handing them each a water. "Isn't Bill supposed to be here working with you?"

"Yeah," one of the students replied, pointing down the hall. "He's . . . over that way, cleaning the bathroom. Well . . . *kind of.*"

Kind of? I followed her direction and soon understood what she meant: Bill was scrubbing a toilet slower than I'd ever seen anyone clean anything in my life. He was standing hunched over, pushing his brush at a snail's pace around the rim, the bristles barely touching the bowl.

"How's it going, Bill?" I asked, hoping the sudden appearance of his boss might inspire him to pick up the pace. But he barely acknowledged me. The only sound I heard came from the sweat dripping off his forehead and splashing into the toilet water.

"Are you okay?" I asked, slightly concerned.

"I'm all right," he said with a big sigh. "Just sick of cleaning bathrooms."

My heart sank. Bill didn't have to tell me he'd rather be anywhere else than that apartment—the zombielike expression on his face said it all. He had already quit on me once before (as a proud member of The 45), and I was sure I was moments away from losing him again.

We needed Bill. We were in the middle of one of those do-or-die days with more apartments to clean than people to do the work. I had to do something to bring him back to life—and pronto.

Do I tell him to hustle? Bribe him with a snack? Grab the toilet brush out of his hand and whack him with it?

None of those options felt right, so I decided to try a different approach. I mentally transported myself back to my high school cheerleading days, and with game day–level enthusiasm, gave Bill a pep talk worthy of a locker room after a disappointing first half.

"You know what, Bill?" I said. "I'm *so* glad you are on our team! Seriously. I don't know what we'd do without you."

Caught off guard, Bill looked up.

"Really?" he asked skeptically.

"Yes, really!" I replied. He started to crack a smile.

"I know bathroom duty can be the absolute worst," I continued, "but thanks for hanging in there."

As I spoke, Bill began to stand up a little straighter, and a small grin slowly spread across his face. It was like he was waking up from the dead. Whatever was happening, I had to keep it going.

"Twist that brush round the bowl, Bill! Spin it like a helicopter!" I began clapping and doing a little shuffle in the doorway as I remixed a hip-hop throwback. Next thing I knew, Bill was jokingly dancing in front of the toilet, spinning the brush in the bowl to the beat. He was laughing. *I* was laughing. Over the top? Probably. Corny? Oh yeah. But suddenly there was energy in that apartment where before there had been only mildew and bleach fumes.

As soon as our dance party ended, Bill went back to work. But this time he was like Mr. Clean himself, scrubbing faster than I'd spent my business loan.

Later that day, I ran into Bill again in another unit. Since I'd seen him last, he had powered through *five* more apartment bathrooms.

"Check out the one next door," he said proudly. "Worst I've ever seen. But I made that baby shine!" Then he asked if he could extend his shift by an hour.

It looked like Bill wouldn't be resigning anytime soon.

That was the summer I became head of the Student Maid cheer squad. Throw a few "rah-rahs" at someone losing steam, and, like Bill, they'd stick around. Heck, they might even forget about the soap and scum and mold and crusty substances and . . . you get the idea.

Of course, my killer dance moves and megaphone couldn't keep everyone excited about a cleaning job. I wasn't (quite) that naive. Some people just weren't cut out for this kind of work. For a few, Student Maid was the first time they had ever cleaned *anything*. (Like . . . in their lives.) All it took was one moldy shower or surprise roach sighting to make them realize they'd rather work retail. And then there was the natural turnover resulting from my genius decision to hire only students, who eventually graduated, found internships, or went home for the summer. But for everyone else, the ones who *weren't* frightened by softball-sized dust bunnies and didn't plan to leave town anytime soon, I was convinced that putting some extra pep in my step was the key to keeping them from quitting.

My new goal: I wanted everyone so excited about their jobs that they danced in the bathrooms with toilet scrubbers *all the time*. Why wait until someone needed a boost or was on the verge of walking out, as Bill had been? I began using every opportunity imaginable to pump up the volume: I ended routine conversations about shift changes with "Keep up the good work!" or "You rock!" When they submitted their time records for payroll, I replied with "YOU'RE AMAZING!!!!!!!!!!!!!!!!!!!!!!!!!!" I would have hired a skywriter to spell out "I ♥ U" over their apartments if I'd had the money. Anything to make people feel great.

In the days before I grounded my helicopter and empowered students to be more self-reliant—back when I was still making those terrible lists for Erin and Abby and telling everyone exactly how to do their jobs—I used to inspect jobsites while students cleaned. The idea was that I'd catch any mistakes they might make before our clients did. It was also the perfect chance to cheer on the team in person. Just as I had with Bill, I told every student I encountered during inspections just how much I appreciated having them at Student Maid. If I sensed anyone's energy flagging even slightly, I gave them a boost with a few complimentary words and a high five, and if I noticed they weren't mopping the floor well or they were making the beds wrong, I gave them . . . an extra high five. Sure, I could have shown them the right way. But why rain on their parade over such a little thing? Instead, I'd wait until they moved on to the next room and then redo the job myself. Simple.

Call me crazy, but my spirit fingers were working. Not only were people still around, but they called in sick less and took on extra shifts more. Many referred their friends to work for us. Life at Student Maid was good, and I figured my cheering had a lot to do with it. I couldn't risk my routines getting stale, so I constantly had my eyes and ears open for fresh moves.

In an article that caught my attention, I read about a leader who came to work each morning with five pennies in his right pocket. Throughout the day, he made it his goal to praise five people, and each time he did, he would move one penny from his right pocket to his left. He didn't leave work until his right pocket was empty, which meant he had met his daily requirement. That sparked an idea: Why didn't I make it *my* goal to recognize *every* student on our team *every single day*? (Checkmate, five-penny-trick man.)

Every morning I printed out a roster of our team members, attached it to a clipboard, and carried it with me at all times. (You think lugging around a rolling briefcase is obnoxious? Try having a clipboard glued to your arm.) Throughout the day, I'd work down the list, reaching out to one student after another with greeting-card-worthy messages of gratitude and encouragement, checking off names as I went. I'd text or say things like "I'm so lucky you are on the team!" or "Thanks for your hard work today, dustbuster!" My friends teased me mercilessly about my dorky clipboard. But every smile or smiley-face emoji I got in response to my expressions of appreciation made the teasing I endured worth it.

Nothing anyone could do would take the cheerleader out of me. No matter what our students did, I found a reason to celebrate and let them know how much they meant to me and how much Student Maid needed them.

Except Courtney.

I had just one thing to say to her: Bring. It. *On*.

—

Just when I thought Courtney couldn't possibly top her impromptu piano recital, she proved me wrong.

A few weeks after that incident, as I was circling the business incubator's parking lot one morning searching for a spot, I noticed something that made me do a double take. Off to my left was a parked car with the phrase BLOW ME scrawled across its back window in huge letters.

Blow me?! Whose car is that? This is an office building, for crying out loud. Only professionals park here . . . and our stud—

Oh no.

You've got to be kidding me.

I knew exactly whose car it was.

As I thought about Courtney driving that vulgar phrase to our clients' homes and parking it in their driveways, something in me snapped. In a way, it felt like her car was talking to *me*.

I whipped into a space, flung open my door, hopped out, and quickly slammed the door shut. As I marched through the incubator, the image of BLOW ME flashing through my head, I happened to catch sight of Courtney grabbing some cleaning rags.

"Good morning!" she practically sang.

"Good" morning? We'll see about that! I thought, throwing her a tight-lipped smile. *Just you wait . . .*

I made a beeline for my desk, dropped dramatically into my chair, took a deep breath, and prepared myself to . . . power up my computer. Someone was about to get a very stern *email*.

With Courtney standing just feet from my office, my fingers flew over my keyboard as I wrote her the harshest message I could, then deleted it and started over. By the time I clicked "send," this is what I'd come up with:

TO: Courtney

SUBJECT: Important

A little birdie told me it says "BLOW ME" on the back of your car. I realize that you probably did not write this, but that needs to be off your back windshield immediately. If a client came home and saw that, what would they think? Please make sure to take it off before your next job. Thank you so much!

Yep, I sure told her, all right—from behind a computer screen while she was physically so close to me I could hear her phone ding as she got the "new message" notification. Then I hid in my office until she left.

Courtney ended up quitting a couple weeks later.

Good riddance, right? Well, yes. And no. In a way, I was relieved that Courtney was gone. Magically, the problem had disappeared.

But it also kind of sucked. I mean, she'd *quit* on me. Courtney was one of those students willing to clean to pay her rent. She drove me nuts, but I needed her, just as I needed everyone else on the team. That was the only reason I'd put up with all her nonsense to begin with and why I couldn't resist giving her a hug instead of giving her hell the first time I tried to confront her.

I praised Courtney, like everyone else, so she wouldn't quit. I ignored her poor choices so she wouldn't quit. Then, when I just couldn't ignore them anymore, I "talked" to her in the nicest, least confrontational way possible . . . so she wouldn't quit.

And she still quit.

Lesson learned: Keep my mouth shut and my fingers off the keyboard. It would be pom-poms only from here on out.

(Guess how well that worked out?)

—

I had mastered the "cheer" part of cheerleader, but I still had a long way to go on the "leader" part.

Fortunately, there was no better place for a rookie leader than the incubator.

When I first signed the lease, I thought my monthly payment of $96 and change was getting me just a place to set up some desks and store our cleaning supplies. What I ended up with was worth so much more.

Every Tuesday morning, the other incubating entrepreneurs and I would meet to talk about things that were (and weren't) going well in each of our businesses. It made me feel less alone to be around people who, like me, were learning how to build a company from the ground up. But the best part about the incubator was that it also came with incredible mentors. Eager to learn, our entrepreneurial posse would gather in the conference room with our laptops open, frantically taking notes as HR professionals, lawyers, former CFOs, and business strategists imparted their years of wisdom to us. They did presentations on budgeting, customer service, and everything in between, all to help us succeed.

The mentors spent a lot of one-on-one time with us too. The first time we met over coffee, Eva, the HR expert, almost spit out her latte when I revealed that my solution to addressing our students' shortcomings was to tell them how great they were and look the other way. After that, Eva never let me out of her sight again.

She was determined to get me to do things "real" companies were supposed to do (and to keep me out of future lawsuits). She wanted me to start by documenting performance and conducting regular employee evaluations.

Well, *that* sounded like the worst idea ever.

The incident with Courtney was still fresh in my mind. Although I wasn't exactly sure why she had resigned, I had a feeling it was because of that "tough" email I'd sent her. That only added to the list of excuses I made to Eva for why I couldn't do evaluations. Our team members already put up with low wages and spent half their workdays elbow deep in toilet water, I told her. Giving them critical feedback on top of that, I thought, would be the last straw. I was sure it would prompt an exodus even greater than the exit of The 45.

Eva wasn't letting me off the hook that easily. She had a counterpoint for every one of my arguments. Deep down, she told me, people really want to know how they're doing at work. She said I couldn't let my fear of people leaving keep them in the dark about their performance, and if I didn't address the issues, they'd inevitably get worse.

The more I listened to Eva, the more I thought about Courtney. And the more I thought about Courtney, the clearer the picture got.

I had been so busy worrying about how Courtney's behavior was affecting Student Maid and me that I had failed to think about the consequences of *my* behavior. Praising her when she was doing the wrong thing didn't help her, the company, or me. I'm pretty sure Student Maid was the first job Courtney ever had. If I had said something to her the second she tried on those Jimmy Choos, maybe she would have thought twice before doing something out of line the next time. Maybe she would have become the best team member we ever had. . . . Okay, probably not. But at least I would've given her the chance to try.

Slowly I was beginning to understand: Giving a pep talk can be powerful. But there's a time for pep talks and a time for reality checks. And a good leader knows when and how to give both. Giving people room to make mistakes doesn't mean excusing bad behavior, ignoring poor decisions, or avoiding the feedback they need to hear to be better. Teaching people to problem-solve on their own is important, but so is helping them grow from their mistakes. If they don't realize they're doing something wrong to begin with, someone has to tell them.

That someone was me.

—

When I finally agreed to give this whole evaluation thing a whirl, Eva jumped in with instructions for my next steps before I could even blink. (It's like she thought I was going to chicken out and change my mind or something.)

She suggested I meet with each student at least once a

semester and go over two things: (1) where they needed to improve and (2) what they were doing well. (Thank goodness for number 2.) She also gave me a few evaluation templates to choose from, but they included words like "candidate" and "supervisor"—a little too official for someone who called her team members "homies."

I used Eva's material as a starting point and came up with my own rubric to assess performance instead. I decided I'd score our students on things like "Cleaning skills are high quality," "Sticks with difficult work until it's done," and "Doesn't drive around with 'blow me' on their car window." (Kidding, but you get the idea.) I rated their ability to meet the criteria on a scale of one to five, and if they got below a five, I'd jot down a few notes as to why. ("You can't make a king bed with twin sheets!")

After I scored everyone and wrote down exactly what needed to be said to them, it was time for an intern to give the students their evaluations. Yes. An *intern*. (Okay, so I did chicken out.) If the recipient of a poor evaluation ended up hating the person who delivered it to them, better it be the intern than me. The interns were there for only a semester and then they never had to see our students again. Not to mention the invaluable HR experience they would gain by conducting evaluations. (Like I would know.) It was the perfect plan . . . until the next semester, when no one signed up for our internship program. Gee. I wonder why?

With no interns available, I thought about asking Erin and Abby to do the evaluations. But the thought of *them* not coming back the next semester was all it took for me to ditch that idea. Reluctantly I took over the job.

In the days leading up to my evaluation debut, panic slowly started creeping in. I wouldn't have a screen to hide behind; I would be face-to-face with our students. My face had to tell their face what they sucked at. I'd rather spray bleach in my eyes than do that. The only way I could live with myself, I decided, was if I figured out how to have these conversations in a way that ensured students left my office with smiles on their faces and love for Student Maid in their hearts—even after they learned they had some things to work on.

The first sit-down evaluation I had slated was with a student who wasn't sharing the driving responsibility fairly with his cleaning partners. (Our students usually clean in teams of two and are required to carpool together, so we ask them to switch up who drives for each shift.) Other than this one issue, he was an amazing team member, and I wanted to make sure he knew it. So I decided to highlight what he did well before I told him he needed to help more with the driving. Then I'd finish on another high note so he'd be less likely to email me his resignation as soon as he walked out my door. Turns out, this method is a pretty common one, and I didn't actually invent it. You may know it as the "shit sandwich." Wish it had a more elegant name, but at least it gets the job done.

The sandwich I served him that day went like this:

Start with something nice: "Thanks so much for coming in to meet with me! I first want to say how appreciative

I am that you picked up several last-minute shifts this semester. It seems like whenever we are in a bind, you're the
one who saves the day."

Sandwich in the "shitty" part: "I also want to bring up
something I need your help with. It's my understanding that
your partners are doing most of the driving each time you
work together, and as you know, we encourage everyone to
share that responsibility. I think it would be more fair to
your coworkers if you offered to drive at least half the time."

End with something even nicer: "I'm telling you this because I care about you and consider you an asset to our
team. Thanks in advance for pitching in more with the driving and for all the other ways you're already contributing to
our company."

Not bad.

Though I never looked forward to evaluations, shit sandwiches made them easier to conduct. (Easier, yes, but not as
effective as they could've been: I'd later learn an even better
approach to giving feedback that would blow my sandwiches off the serving platter. But we'll get to that later.)
The more practice I got at delivering sandwiches, the more
comfortable I became handing them out.

It soon occurred to me that I shouldn't wait until evaluations to give out constructive feedback. Once I'd greenlit
students to try to figure out things on their own and stopped
inspecting jobsites (i.e., secretly cleaning up after people), it
wasn't uncommon for customers to come home and find
mistakes. While most of our students thrived with their
newfound independence and made our customers happy, let

me paint a picture of what some of the others were doing: Forgetting to set house alarms, helping pets escape by leaving a door open while taking out the trash (we always found them!), mopping *blinds* (for real). Instead of getting phone calls from our students asking me to solve their challenges on the job, I was now fielding complaints from customers, including one who told me her house would've gotten cleaned better if she'd paid her ten-year-old to do it instead. (Burn.) We frequently gave out discounts to keep our reputation from going down the drain, but I knew that was only a Band-Aid solution to a problem that seemed to be getting bigger by the day. Giving a $25 refund to a client every time the same student forgot to vacuum the stairs was adding up. It suddenly seemed foolish to wait until evaluations to remind a student that stairs get dirty too. So instead of handing out increasingly steep discounts to customers, I started giving out more timely sandwiches to students.

Most took their good-with-the-bad feedback like champs and immediately improved, but others, I found, just couldn't seem to handle these conversations. For a few of our team members, even something minor, like asking them to be better about wiping baseboards, could open the tear floodgates. On some rare occasions I even got emails from their parents—those same overhelping moms and dads—who wanted to know why I'd dared to criticize their twenty-year-old "child's" dusting techniques. (Oy vey.) Some students were so scared of getting a sandwich that they avoided me at all costs. If it wasn't time for evaluations and I asked them to meet with me in my office, they'd make all kinds of excuses as to why they couldn't or ask me to email them whatever I had to say instead. Some simply responded to my meeting requests with "Am I getting fired?" (All this time I'd thought criticism would make our students quit, and here it was making them think they were losing their jobs.)

There's a reason many of our students were so sensitive to criticism (and why they responded so well to my over-the-top praise and cheer routines). It's not for nothing that millennials are nicknamed the "Participation Generation." As kids, many of us got rewarded just for showing up: We got trophies in soccer even if we sat on the bench all season; we got stickers when we got A's *and* when we got C's; we got ribbons even when we came in last place. The message from teachers, coaches, and parents alike was "You're great. You're special. Go you."

This isn't true of every millennial in my company. (And it's not a problem confined to a single generation either—plenty of nonmillennials struggle with feedback too.) But I believe a big part of why it was so exceptionally hard for some of our students to handle criticism does have to do with the special-snowflake status they had growing up. When people who have been raised this way get to the workplace, it's very likely that their first performance review (or shit sandwich) is the first time they've been given real, honest feedback. And when you've been told you're the bee's knees your whole life, you're not really sure how to handle it when your boss informs you that you kind of suck at something.

I thought back to the shepherd's pie days, when I watched

my team struggle to fix their mistakes. As hard as that was, keeping my distance allowed our students to become more confident problem solvers. Giving critical feedback might be uncomfortable for me, and getting it might be hard for our students, but I suspected that, similarly, it would be the best thing for all of us. In the end, they'd gain greater self-awareness, which would benefit them not only in this job but in every job they had afterward.

And wouldn't you know: The more sandwich-style conversations we had, the less the students avoided them. Those who initially had a tough time with them finally understood I wasn't trying to crush them by pointing out their weaknesses; I just wanted to help them succeed. And in return, they wanted to help Student Maid (and themselves) by improving.

But in case you're like I was and are still hesitant about hopping aboard the feedback ferry, I'll be your Eva and give you a push: A survey of millennials featured in a 2015 *Forbes* article reported that almost 90 percent said they would feel more confident if they received frequent or ongoing feedback at work. And a 2014 survey published in the *Harvard Business Review* showed that a whopping 72 percent of employees—from all generations—said they thought their careers would benefit from more corrective feedback as well.

See? Feedback is *good*. It just gets a bad rap from people (like me) who used to be afraid of it.

I was finally getting somewhere, both with students and with myself as a leader: My clipboard in one hand and a sandwich in the other, I felt like I'd struck the right balance between making our students feel good and telling them when they needed to be better. No one was quitting. The crying was subsiding. I was reaching around to pat myself on the back.

But, as the story usually goes, I'd soon find I had a lot more to learn.

—

After almost two years in the incubator, Student Maid had grown more than I could have ever dreamed.

We were one of the lucky ones: While some of the other entrepreneurs in the building came to the painful realization that their companies just weren't going to work, we were bursting at the seams. We had more people working for us than any start-up there. It was becoming disruptive to have our students walking in and out, clanking vacuums and brooms as the other tenants attempted to make important calls and conduct meetings. We needed our own place.

By this point, we were making enough money to splurge a little. We signed a lease for our very own pad. With four rooms, plus a common area and a big warehouse to store supplies, it was a palace compared with our 450-square-foot office space at the incubator. I gave Erin and Abby each a small raise, and I even treated myself to the occasional pair of denim. We were far from making millions—like, super-duper far—but for a business that had unintentionally started with a Craigslist ad, it wasn't too shabby.

I was ecstatic about our growth, but I was also petrified.

Now that we were out of the incubator, it felt real. Our new lease was a three-year agreement, and as I dotted my i's and crossed my t's, I remembered something I'd read about most businesses failing within the first five years. Even though Student Maid was doing just dandy at the time, I couldn't help but feel added pressure to make sure we continued on that path. I'd learned from the mentors at the incubator that the best thing I could do for our long-term success was work *on* the business instead of *in* it, so that's what I set out to do.

With Erin and Abby handling day-to-day operations, I spent as much time as possible networking in the community and going to every meeting that I could fit in my day planner, all to find new clients and contracts. When I was in the office, I was on the phone following up on sales leads rather than greeting students as they passed through on the way to and from shifts. I'd managed to keep up with my clipboard-and-sandwich routine after our big move, but my time was increasingly limited, and I knew that eventually something would have to give. I didn't feel right putting feedback-dishing duties on Erin or Abby, and truthfully, part of me still didn't trust anyone else to handle such a sensitive matter. So I sacrificed my clipboard (RIP, Clippy), boxed up my pom-poms, and told Erin and Abby that they were now responsible for keeping up morale around the office while I remained on sandwich duty.

Turns out, letting my pom-poms collect dust was a bad move. Things at Student Maid started to change. When I saw our team members in passing, I noticed that people looked down in the dumps instead of upbeat, and they weren't hanging around after their shifts anymore. They'd even started to call out of work more often. When a few students who had been with us for a long time resigned out of the blue, I knew something was really wrong. They never gave me specific reasons for their resignations—just that they were ready for something different. I knew the real reason, though: Student Maid had gone from rah-rah to blah. It was my worst fear coming to life.

At first I blamed it on Erin and Abby. *How could they let this happen?* I thought. Every chance I got, I reminded them how important it was to keep praise and appreciation flowing. I'd assumed they were natural-born cheerleaders like me. But through no fault of their own, they weren't.

What I needed to do was clear: I had to figure out a way to keep everyone positive and motivated even when I wasn't around.

Thank goodness I was about to meet Rich. If it hadn't been for him, we might have been one of those businesses that fail in their first five years.

—

Rich Blaser and I crossed paths at a mixer for local start-ups and investors.

I wasn't there looking for an investor; I was there in search of some new business buddies. Being out of the incubator meant I was no longer working alongside other entrepreneurs every day—or having HR coffee chats with Eva—and I was starting to feel pretty lonely. Anytime I heard about an event like this one, I was the first to sign up.

I was desperate to meet people I could relate to, confide in, and talk to about Student Maid's growing pains.

When I met Rich on this particular evening, he told me all about how he and his friend Darin had started their company, Infinite Energy, twenty years earlier when they were both fresh out of college. I thought *I* had it rough, but it took these guys *two years* of trying before they got their first business loan. Whoever finally took a chance on them, though, could breathe easy. The company was now a major success. It had four hundred employees, sold natural gas and electricity to 125,000 customers in five states, and was bringing in more than $600 million in sales per year.

Rich was my kind of guy. First, he was wearing jeans. Second, I found out his company had been voted one of the best places to work in Florida several times in a row (my dream). As Rich and I chatted, we discovered we had one very big thing in common: We both believed our companies were better because of the people in them. But more than that, we wanted our people to be better because they worked for our companies. I was pretty sure a guy like Rich already had plenty of business pals, but maybe he had room for one more.

Turns out he was thinking the same thing. On our way out of the event, Rich gave me an invitation I couldn't turn down. He was putting together a group of young entrepreneurs whom he would meet with once a month to coach, and he wanted to know if I was interested in being a part of it.

Interested? It was only exactly what I was looking for.

The format was simple: At each meeting, six of us (including Rich) took turns sharing what was going well for us and what wasn't. If we brought up something we were struggling with, the others would chime in and offer solutions until we felt we could move on to the next challenge. It felt a lot like the Tuesday-morning meetings at the incubator, except these lasted four or five hours, and everyone Rich invited to participate owned a business that was growing at about the same pace.

Before one of our first meetings, Rich gave us an unforgettable tour of Infinite Energy's campus (yes, a campus; it's that big). As we meandered through the different departments and divisions, I couldn't believe how *happy* people were. When we got to the sales floor, I spotted a group of four or five people congregated in front of what looked like a scoreboard. They were smiling and laughing and patting one another on the back. I wasn't sure what they were so excited about, but their energy brought me back to the day a couple years before when Bill (aka Mr. Clean) and I had danced in that apartment bathroom. Rich explained that the scoreboard tracked sales goals and that I was witnessing the celebration of a team that had hit theirs.

The magic didn't happen only on the sales floor: As we toured other buildings, Rich introduced us to employees, many of whom told us they had been with the company for ten, fifteen, even twenty years. Some said they loved their jobs so much that they'd brought their spouses and children on board to work at Infinite Energy as well. Not so long ago our students had referred their friends to work at Student Maid all the time—but that was back when I had more time for cheering and our students loved their jobs a lot more than they appeared to love them now.

It didn't make sense. Rich and Darin had *hundreds* of employees. If I didn't have time to recognize everyone in my company every day, Rich and Darin couldn't possibly have time for that either. During our campus tour, Rich admitted he didn't even *know* all his employees. Yet everyone I encountered at Infinite Energy seemed infinitely happy. How was that possible? Forget Gen-Y Kool-Aid. I wanted whatever Rich had on tap.

When we got back to the conference room for our meeting, I remember looking at Rich and thinking how grateful I was to have the chance to learn from someone like him. I hoped that maybe if I followed in his footsteps, Student Maid could become half the company Infinite Energy was one day.

Right off the bat, Rich emphasized how much he had learned about leadership from reading. He encouraged each of us to become avid readers ourselves and suggested we start by picking up one of his favorite books: Patrick Lencioni's *The Three Signs of a Miserable Job* (which has since been renamed *The Truth About Employee Engagement*).

In the book, Lencioni identifies three things that can cause people to have miserable work experiences: immeasurement (not having an immediate, concrete way to measure their performance); anonymity (not feeling appreciated by their leaders for their contributions); and irrelevance (not knowing what difference their work makes or why it matters).

Thanks to Rich's book suggestion, I could finally pinpoint

the real reason The 45 had walked out on me. When I sat in that comfy armchair in the clubhouse, I wasn't measuring anyone's performance. I wasn't telling anyone I valued them. I wasn't giving them any reason to believe that their scrubbing and scraping was meaningful in any way. I was giving them a miserable job. I probably would have quit too.

I also understood better now why my cheerleading had been so effective when I had the time for it. Every time I told our students how thankful I was to have them on the team, they felt appreciated instead of anonymous. When I told them how much their hard work mattered to me and the team, they felt needed instead of irrelevant. No wonder misery crept in the moment I put my cheerleading routine on hold.

But even when I was doing all that in full force, the feel-good level at Student Maid paled in comparison with what I witnessed at Infinite Energy. And not because they had a campus and we had four rooms and a warehouse. Rich and his team had found a way to combat each one of Lencioni's three signs, even as the company grew.

I had to figure out how to do the same.

—

I couldn't wait to share everything I read in Lencioni's book with Erin and Abby. Almost immediately, we started brainstorming how we could cast out misery from Student Maid for good.

We started by tackling immeasurement. In his book, Lencioni talks about giving a cashier at a restaurant a concrete way to measure one aspect of her work—customer satisfaction—in real time. It was simple: Every day she would count the number of smiles she got from customers, which helped her track her performance. Doing so made her work hard to increase the number of smiles she got every day. Something like counting smiles seemed so simple, but it wouldn't work at Student Maid. Unlike in the restaurant business—and most service businesses—our students have minimal customer interaction. Clients usually aren't home at the time of service, and if it's a commercial client, cleaning usually happens after hours, when everyone in the building has gone home. The only way our students knew how well (or not-so-well) they did was if *I* told them. And the only way I could tell them was if the clients told Erin and Abby and then Erin and Abby told me.

In response to the challenge of figuring out how to get feedback from our clients directly to our students, we created a survey. The survey, which we emailed to our customers immediately following their cleanings, included four different performance ratings—poor, good, excellent, and perfect—as well as a box for our clients to explain their scores. Whenever a survey, good or bad, came back to the office, we forwarded it along to the team responsible so they could track their performance. I wish I could say we got every survey back every time, but let's be real. Our clients are busy humans with busy lives. If we were lucky, we got back 60 percent of the surveys. But that was 60 percent more information about performance than we had before. *Hasta la vista*, immeasurement.

The surveys had another benefit we weren't expecting: Our clients used them to tell our students the impact their work had on them. In the comment box, they'd write about the ways in which our cleaning teams were making a difference in their lives. Rather than spending their evenings straightening up, they could now spend that time with their kids. Or when they had a dinner party, their guests commented on how great the place looked. Some even told us we saved their marriage. (Fighting over chores can get heated.) And just like that, we said good-bye to irrelevance too.

There was just one more sign of a miserable job to tackle, and it was a toughie: anonymity.

We had to come up with a way to recognize our students that worked with or without my participation. That's when I remembered the scene on the sales floor at Infinite Energy: Rich's employees crowded around a scoreboard, looking at their results and cheering for one another's accomplishments. Rich wasn't standing there with them—he was giving us a tour of his campus. His employees didn't need him there to feel acknowledged because Rich gave them the opportunity to make one another feel that way.

I can't recall who actually came up with the idea, but either Erin or Abby suggested we display every perfect survey on a wall in our office for *everyone* in the company to see. Our "scoreboard" would look exactly like Rich's fancy, high-tech, flat-screen one . . . except that it'd be made out of construction paper and Crayola markers. We'd call it the "WOW Wall." (The name was definitely my idea.)

A beautiful thing happened after the WOW Wall went

up: The cheerleading spirit that I thought only I could keep alive became contagious. When a student who "made the wall" walked into the office, it seemed natural to Erin and Abby to say "Congratulations!" Other students picked up pom-poms too, celebrating their teammates for impressing our clients. Because those who got perfect ratings could see exactly what our customers raved about, it made them want to keep doing those things to keep their names on the wall. And it made those who were getting less-than-stellar reviews want to improve so that they could be up there one day too. All they had to do was look at the wall to get some ideas of how they could do it.

The WOW Wall, which I passed every time I went to my desk, was a constant reminder that part of my job as a leader was to keep immeasurement, anonymity, and irrelevance at bay. It was also comforting because it reminded me I now had help in fulfilling that charge. The Student Maid cheerleaders were no longer a squad of one. I was confident that no matter how busy I got with other things or how long I was away from the office, the positive energy would still be there when I returned.

How could I have guessed that our customer surveys would soon turn Student Maid into drama central?

—

Now that their performance was being measured and publicly recognized, our students thought twice about whom they were working with. Our best cleaners didn't want to be paired with newer, less experienced team members or those who were "just average." In the past, students had expressed little preference for one cleaning partner over another, and they'd hardly complained about a teammate's performance. But now they'd send me agitated texts begging me to switch the schedule around as soon as they saw Erin and Abby had scheduled them with "Matt the worst mopper" or "Danielle the terrible duster."

I knew what I should do: give shit sandwiches to those who needed improvement and tell our best to take them under their wing instead of huffing and puffing. But there was *no way* I could make all those sandwiches; my arms would have fallen off. Plus, I understood where the high achievers were coming from. (If you've ever been graded on a group project, you probably do too.) They didn't want someone else's dusting or mopping deficiencies keeping them off the WOW Wall. So I took the easy way out and gave our students exactly what they asked for. When they grumbled about their cleaning partners, I told Erin and Abby to avoid that pairing at all costs in the future.

Of course, this approach quickly caught up with me. Thanks to my new partner-pairing restrictions, we hardly had anyone we could schedule to work together. Not only that, but now that I'd basically told everyone I'd take care of their issues for them, I was getting messages about all sorts of interoffice drama. Students were even coming to me when they had complaints about Erin or Abby. I was right back in the middle of solving everyone's problems again. Great.

At my next meeting with Rich and the group, I asked (begged) for advice.

"Why is everyone coming to you with their frustrations instead of the person they are actually upset with?" Rich asked me.

Good question. Because I let them.

As we brainstormed ideas and potential solutions, I told the group about shit sandwiches and how they had worked for me back when there wasn't so much . . . *shit*. One of the group members recommended I look into 360-degree reviews: They were kind of like the evaluations Eva had encouraged me to do, except in addition to getting feedback from me—"the boss"—each student would also be evaluated by their coworkers and those they reported to, which in this case meant Erin and Abby. In addition, the students would assess their *own* performance as well as that of their teammates, Erin, Abby, and me. The goal was for each person to end up with a holistic view of how they were doing in their role. Because complaints about people in the company were coming at me from every angle, 360-degree reviews sounded promising.

When the group offered an idea I wanted to implement, I often had to adapt it to make it work with our unique business model. The person who suggested the 360-degree reviews said that at his company people did them in small groups of three or four and that they were always done face-to-face. Our students worked with dozens of different partners, and because of everyone's class schedules and extracurriculars, it was impossible to get more than a couple of people together in the same room at the same time, so that wasn't going to work for us.

I decided to conduct our 360-degree reviews in the form of an online survey. (We were big on surveys in those days.) Each student would start by reflecting on their own cleaning performance. What did they do well? Where did they need to step up their game? Then they'd score anyone they had worked with before: The survey listed every person on our team with a spot for their cleaning quality to be ranked on a scale from one to ten and another spot for the survey taker to answer "If you ranked this person below a 10, how can they improve?" There was another section for them to rate Erin, Abby, and me and comment on how we were doing as leaders. I kept the survey anonymous with the hope that they'd feel safe going #nofilter and actually say to each other what they were texting and emailing me. After everyone had entered their responses (within a specified window of time), each person would get an email with only their individual results, including feedback from Erin, Abby, and me.

When it came time to read my own results, I was surprised to find myself a little (a lot) nervous. Erin and Abby were sweating it too. This was the first time our students had had the chance to give *us* feedback on our performance. I mean, I didn't think anyone could possibly have anything bad to say about *me* (head cheerleader, remember?), but there was only one way to find out.

I started reading.

First survey: 10/10. "No complaints! You're great, Kristen!"

Hallelujah. I breathed a deep sigh of relief.

The next few looked a lot like the first. But then:

Fifth survey: 6/10. "You park too close to the door and it's not fair. We have to carry our cleaning supplies farther and that really sucks when we're short on time or it's raining outside."

I will never park there again. Ever.

Ninth survey: 7/10. "You are too nice. You let people walk all over you."

Ouch.

Eleventh survey: 5/10. "Way too nice to people. You shouldn't give them everything they want."

Things did not go as the head cheerleader had anticipated they would. By the end, my average was scarily close to a 5/10. I found myself wishing I had a glass of wine even though it was nine A.M.

"Well, this was *terrible*!" I shouted across the hall to Erin and Abby.

"We are *never* doing this again," Erin yelled.

"Ever!" Abby added.

—

Despite my horror as I read my evaluations, I soon realized that the survey had done its job and then some.

Things quieted down for me in the weeks after the results came out. Not one student ended up with a perfect review—not even our best cleaners—and after realizing that they all had areas to improve, they let up on the partner blacklist requests and on their complaints about Erin and Abby. Giving them all the chance to air their concerns about one another meant that I was no longer the dumping ground for those frustrations and resentments.

The truth is, the students had more to say than I had even realized, not just about one another and Erin and Abby, but also about me. It made sense. All that time I was dishing out sandwiches, I wasn't giving anyone the chance to serve me a plate. If I was genuinely committed to becoming a better leader, I needed to grow with the feedback the students had for me too. Clearly I had some things to work on, and I vowed to get started right away.

After the 360-degree reviews, I stopped parking by the door. (To this day I still park in the farthest spot, even if there's a hurricane outside.) And the "you're too nice" comments? There were a lot more of those. I hadn't realized the team knew I was granting partner-pairing wishes left and right like a fairy freaking godmother, but it was good to know they were paying attention, because now I would never let it happen again. Erin and Abby learned about things they could be doing better as well, and they too took their results to heart and worked to address them.

Our 360-degree reviews proved to be so valuable that we did them a couple times a year. Each time we got back our results, we all learned more about how we could be better teammates and leaders, and we got more comfortable accepting and working on where we needed to improve.

The reviews were what made me realize that leaders need regular, candid feedback too. And I know it was *just* a survey and not exactly revolutionary, but it was significant because it was the first time we'd given our students a tool for evaluating us and those they worked with. The only down-side was that they did it from behind a computer screen.

The WOW Wall had helped our students cheer one an-other on in person, but I hadn't yet figured out how to help people get comfortable giving feedback face-to-face. So for many years, anonymous online surveys were how we han-dled confrontation at Student Maid.

Until that one day the FBI showed up.

—

Remember how I said I'd learn something one day that would blow my sandwiches off the serving platter? This is that part.

Bob Chapman is the CEO of Barry-Wehmiller, a $3 bil-lion capital equipment and engineering company based in St. Louis with more than twelve thousand employees world-wide. We met when I was invited to speak at an intimate conference he hosted at his ranch in Aspen, many years after I introduced the sandwich method for feedback at Stu-dent Maid. If I weren't running my own company, I'd want to work for Bob Chapman. If you were to ask him about his company, he wouldn't start by talking about the machines they build. Instead he'd say, "We measure our success by the way we touch the lives of others, and that comes through in everything we do."

I love Barry-Wehmiller because everything it does is about helping its people thrive. For years, the company has offered a communications course that is known for dramatically changing the interpersonal relationships of Barry-Wehmiller's team members—not just at work, but also at home. In fact, the class was so successful that Chapman and his team decided to create a powerful three-day training and offer it to those outside the company through an entity called the Barry-Wehmiller Learning Institute. Since the course's inception, more than ten thousand people from inside and outside Barry-Wehmiller have taken the class, called Listen Like a Leader, and I am fortunate enough to be one of them. This is where I learned all about the FBI—no, not *that* FBI. In this case, the FBI is an approach to giving feedback that is light-years beyond the sandwich method in terms of effectiveness.

The class helped me understand that the problem with the way most people give feedback—whether it's sandwiched between positive affirmations or not—is that we don't deliver it in a way that inspires the recipient to change their behavior. Barry-Wehmiller teaches that if you want to give truly effective feedback, you need to communicate three things: the way you feel, the specific behavior that made you feel that way, and the impact that behavior has—whether it's on you, the company, your relationship with that person, or anything else.

Feeling-Behavior-Impact. F. B. I.

Here's an example of an FBI statement: "I feel disappointed that you were thirty minutes late to the meeting yesterday afternoon, and now I'm unsure if I can rely on you in the future."

Let's break down its awesomeness.

Feeling: The more you can focus on how *you* feel and not on how you perceive the other person feels, the less the person on the receiving end can dispute your statement. For example, if someone's late and you tell them, "You don't care about your responsibility," you open the door to argumentative and defensive responses: *That's not true. I do care!* If you say, "I feel angry," "I feel frustrated," or "I feel disappointed," you leave little room for debate.

Behavior: The recipient needs to know what they did that caused you to feel a certain way, and the more specific you can be, the better. If you were to say simply, "You were late," that person might have trouble pinpointing an exact instance of the behavior, especially if you waited a couple days before talking to them about it.

Impact: People generally don't wake up in the morning and say, "I want to ruin so-and-so's day." They don't usually intend for their behavior to negatively impact anyone or anything. When they know that it has, they will likely try to make sure it doesn't happen again. In this particular example, when you tell someone that their behavior makes you question their reliability, you are showing them the consequences of being late and inspiring them to want to do differently next time.

But wait. *There's more.*

The FBI is also the perfect tool for recognition. I didn't even know there was a *right* way to give recognition. I always thought that as long as I said something, it meant something.

Well, as it turns out, just as vague comments don't help someone change their negative behavior, random praise (like "You're amazing!!!!") doesn't inspire anyone to keep doing great things. We shouldn't praise people just to praise them. It's like the whole Participation Generation thing: If we tell people they are awesome at everything, how will they know what they are really good at? Instead of thanking people for just showing up and doing what is expected of them, we should look for what they do that is above and beyond and acknowledge them for *those* things.

Same deal here. When you recognize someone with an FBI, you tell them how they made you *feel*, the *behavior* that specifically made you feel that way, and the *impact* of their actions. When we give someone all three pieces, they'll usually be inspired to repeat that behavior—again and again and again.

Here's an example: "I felt grateful when you stayed late last night to help me with the report, and it allowed me to make it home in time to put my kids to bed."

Guess who is likely going to volunteer to stay late again the next time you need help?

I learned so many things in the Barry-Wehmiller class, but the FBI takes the cake. It was simple, easy, and effective. I wanted everyone at Student Maid to be an FBI expert. Not because the company was experiencing anything like those drama-filled days from years ago, but because I didn't want our students to have to wait for an online survey to share their concerns. I wanted them to be able to give feedback as soon as they had it, and to know how to deliver their message in person, without hiding behind a screen. Over the next several months, with permission of course, I developed a half-day workshop that incorporated some of the things

I'd learned from Barry-Wehmiller, FBI chief among them. Participation in the class was, and continues to be, a requirement for every single member of our team; they are paid to attend.

Today, not only have FBIs completely replaced the sandwich method at Student Maid, but they've also eliminated the need for anonymous surveys. Because we've taught our students an effective way to confront their peers, they feel empowered to solve interpersonal issues face-to-face. Every person at Student Maid—me, those who lead our company, our students—now has an extremely effective way to give any member of our team corrective feedback, which we encourage them to give in person whenever possible. We literally just walk up to each other and say, "Hey, I need to give you an FBI." It's that simple. So simple, in fact, that our students have chosen to use it outside of work. Take, for example, the student who told me she used an FBI to confront her professor when she felt she was being unfairly picked on in class. After she gave the FBI, the professor stopped teasing her.

FBIs even made me rethink our WOW Wall.

The wall hasn't gone anywhere. It's a lot bigger and fancier now, and it's still a very popular spot in our office. It's still how our students see what our clients are saying about their work. But while many of our customers do fill out the surveys, there are still many who never do. Which means there's a good chance that there are some students who are doing amazing work and not being recognized for it on the wall. It makes me sad to think that in the past, there may have been team members who went home day after day wondering if anyone even noticed their efforts. As it turns out, the WOW Wall was not the perfect solution to the anonymity problem. FBIs, though, are pretty darn close.

FBIs have taught us to acknowledge our students frequently for the ways in which they contribute to our team and the company: picking up a shift last minute, helping us with an errand, unloading the dishwasher in our kitchen. When we see someone carting their cleaning supplies into the office with sweat dripping down their face after a grueling day, we have a way to tell them sincerely how much their hard work means to us. We've even created a second WOW Wall, where team members write FBIs to recognize one another and pin them up for all to see. Our students have also gotten into the habit of giving us—the leaders of the company—FBIs when we go above and beyond (cue the warm and fuzzies). Before FBIs, I imagine some of those leading my company were also going home after work wondering if anyone appreciated their efforts. Today they no longer need to wonder.

If it sounds like now, years later, I finally have it all figured out, I don't. I still struggle constantly with finding the right balance between cheering people on and telling them where they need to improve. Is it the 2:1 ratio of the sandwich? 1:1 to keep it balanced? 5:1 to keep people feeling great? If I give *too much* praise and not enough constructive criticism, will our students turn into special snowflakes again? (These are the things that keep me up at night.)

In one of my favorite books, *The 7 Habits of Highly Ef-*

fective People, Stephen Covey writes about "emotional bank accounts." In every relationship, he says, there is an emotional "balance." If the balance is negative, people feel undervalued. To keep a positive balance, we must have more "deposits" than "withdrawals," just like a real bank account.

At work, recognition counts as a deposit, and critical feedback counts as a withdrawal. Withdrawals are bound to happen and, as we know, are necessary. As long as we are making regular deposits, the balance will stay positive even when we have to take a withdrawal. However, if we keep taking withdrawals without making any deposits, we'll eventually be deducting from a negative balance. This is usually around the time the person on the receiving end decides to move on from the relationship—or in this case the organization—because they feel unappreciated.

So, all this to say: Researchers have done all kinds of studies and come back with all different answers about what the exact balance should be. Despite the lack of consensus, however, they do generally agree that there should be a little more clapping than critiquing. That's a helpful place to begin. (Good news for all the head cheerleaders out there.)

—

As leaders we have the awesome opportunity—and responsibility—to help our people be the best they can be. That means we have to be open and honest about the things they do that let us down. But it also means that we have to keep the pom-poms nearby, get our clipboards ready, and put our WOW Walls front and center.

Anytime I'm tempted to sweep an issue under the rug, I think about Courtney and how I failed her by not giving her feedback and a chance to make better decisions. And anytime I see a student not working to their full potential or looking miserable in their job, I think about Bill and how I brought him back from the living dead by choosing to show him appreciation instead of whacking him with a toilet brush.

To learn, grow, and be successful, people need feedback—the good, the bad, and the ugly. And to thrive, a company needs to provide its people with a system for communicating that feedback effectively at all levels. At Student Maid, that's what FBIs have given us.

So I'll give you one.

I feel grateful that you have made it to the end of this chapter, and the impact it has is that my publisher may just take a chance on another novice writer one day.

(But please, keep reading.)

4 ~~TWO~~ DEAL BREAKERS

I heard a soft knock on my office door.

Nice. Five minutes early.

My two P.M. interview had arrived, and if there was anything I'd learned about hiring people, it was that promptness was an *outstanding* sign.

I did a quick scan of the room. Cell phone on silent? *Yep.* Desk neat and organized? *Of course.* Student Maid energy radiating from my soul? *Isn't it always?* I smiled until I could feel the dimples in both my cheeks, and then opened the door to give our newest applicant a warm welcome.

From the moment I greeted Jade, I knew she was a winner. Upbeat. Solid eye contact. Confident handshake. Button-down shirt . . . with *a blazer.*

"Come on in," I said, pointing to the chair in front of my desk. "Have a seat and make yourself comfortable."

As she settled in, I sat down across from her, pulled my hiring checklist from a drawer, and clicked my favorite pen.

I began with my standard opener: "So, Jade, how'd you hear about Student Maid?"

"A friend of mine told me about it," she said. "I went to your website and I love your story. It's really cool that you started a company for a pair of jeans."

Impressive. She did her research.

"All right, so," I continued, "I see on your résumé that you're studying psychology. What made you choose that as your major?"

"I've always been fascinated with people," she responded, perfectly poised. "I'm not really sure what I want to do with my degree yet, but I love my classes."

Amazing. Our clients are people, so this is just great.

"What about previous work experience?" I asked. "Ever had a job before?"

"Yes," she replied. "I bused tables for three years at a restaurant back home before I moved here for college."

Not afraid to get dirty. And she's loyal! Getting better by the second.

Jade answered the next few questions flawlessly, so I decided she was ready for my signature curveball.

"What's your spirit animal?"

(I didn't say it was a *good* question.)

She thought about it for a moment, as everyone did, and then settled on a giraffe. "They have a unique perspective," she elaborated. "They get to see everything from really high up. You know, the big picture."

Wow. First person to give that one a real answer.

I didn't need to ask Jade another question to know that she was 100 percent Student Maid material. I wanted her to start *yesterday*. But before I could offer her the cleaning job of a lifetime, I had to make sure she met the rest of our requirements. Standard protocol.

"Jade, thanks so much for meeting with me today," I said with a grin. "I've got a couple of quick 'housekeeping' questions to ask, and then we'll get you out of here. We only hire students, and you are a student, so we're good there. Can you tell me your GPA?"

"Three point seven," she replied. "But I'm hoping to get it higher next semester."

No need. Well beyond our 3.5 GPA minimum. Check!

"And what's your availability like?" I hesitated. (This is where I usually lost people.)

"It's pretty open," she said. "I can work any day after one P.M. and anytime on the weekends."

Whew. Better than most. Check!

"And the last one: You have a car, right?"

"Um, well, I don't, actually," she said, looking down. "But I'm saving up for one!" she added quickly.

No, Jade! No! Please tell me I heard that wrong.

"Well, how'd you get here today?" I asked gently. There had to be a way around this.

"I walked," she said.

Walked? Our office is in the middle of nowhere.

I tried to keep my expression neutral as a silent struggle took place in my head.

It's not that important to have a car, right? I can break my own rule just this once—

NO. Don't even think about it. You came up with this checklist for a reason. She has to have a car.

"I'm so sorry, Jade. Unfortunately, I can't hire you until you have a vehicle."

Her shoulders dropped.

Along with my heart.

What did I just do?

———

That night I couldn't sleep.

I tossed and turned as I thought about Jade's interview, wondering if I'd made the right choice. Something in my gut told me I hadn't.

When I woke up the next morning, I *knew* I'd messed up. What had I been thinking? (A question I ask myself a lot.) Jade was exactly the kind of person I wanted representing Student Maid. She had done her research about my company—no one did their research—and the disappointment on her face when I told her I couldn't offer her the job showed how much she had wanted it. Plus, she *walked* to her interview, and presumably home too. If that's not the definition of going the extra mile, then what is?

As I ate my breakfast, I considered all the ways we could make this work: Jade could ride with a coworker, borrow a friend's car, roller-skate, hitchhike. I could schedule her at places close to her apartment. And if I hired her, maybe she'd actually be able to save up for a car. (Duh.) I called Jade as soon as I finished my cereal to surprise her with the news: I was going to give her a job after all.

Well. I was the one who ended up surprised.

Jade told me that when I turned her down, she immediately accepted an offer somewhere else. She had interviewed at a few other places but was holding out for Student Maid because it was the one she wanted most. And now that she had already given another company her commitment, she told me she couldn't go back on her word to them.

That is a person of integrity. A person I should have hired when I had the chance.

I'm not sure if I'll ever be able to forgive myself for letting Jade walk away (literally and figuratively—I still beat myself up for not offering her a ride home). I can't believe I let a stupid rule get in the way of hiring one of the best applicants I'd ever met. But at the same time, I'm thankful for the tough lesson Jade taught me:

My hiring requirements were BS.

—

I created my hiring checklist a couple years before Jade's interview, back when I was still a student myself.

In a marketing class I'd taken, I learned about "competitive advantages." Apparently, if I could find a way to make my company stand out from the other cleaning businesses in town, I'd attract more customers. That's where the first two boxes on my hiring checklist came from: To be eligible for a spot on our team, I decided, the applicant would have to be a student and would also need at least a 3.5 GPA. It worked. People chose to use us over other cleaning companies because they liked the idea that their money would be supporting ambitious, hardworking students. Now, instead of Joe Smith vacuuming your living room, it was Joe Smith, the mechanical engineering major who's studying for his thermodynamics exam whenever he isn't vacuuming your living room.

The third box on the checklist had to do with availability and scheduling. Too often I'd give someone a job only to find out afterward that their availability looked like this: "I can work M, W, F between classes, from nine A.M. to nine thirty A.M." *Greeaaat*. Thirty minutes is about enough time to sweep a kitchen. I was willing to work around everyone's class schedules because I knew school was their priority, but I needed them to be able to clean at least an entire house each time they worked.

Then there was the last box on the checklist, the one that got Jade: having a vehicle. Our students were responsible for transporting themselves and their cleaning supplies to and from jobsites, which were spread across town. Not all clients were located close to bus routes, and this was before Uber became a thing. I couldn't risk our students being late, so I decided they'd need to have their own reliable transportation.

Meeting all four requirements wasn't the only thing they had to do to get a spot on the team, though. That'd be too easy. Even my HR-rookie self knew I had to ask a few questions to make sure the job seeker was the kind of person I wanted representing Student Maid.

I had no clue what I was supposed to ask applicants in interviews, but thankfully Google did. I scoured the Internet and compiled a huge list of questions that looked promising, then narrowed it down to the ten or fifteen I thought were best. Most were pretty standard (and boring), like "Why should I hire you?" and "What do you consider your biggest accomplishment so far, and why?" I also included a few that would shake things up and keep applicants on their toes, like the spirit animal question and "If you were an ice cream flavor, what would you be?"

Sometimes people's answers to my questions made my hiring decisions a breeze.

I will never forget the guy who took an incredibly long time to answer "What's your biggest weakness?"

I interpreted his silence to mean that he was a deep thinker, so I didn't want to interrupt him. But after a few long, quiet minutes I asked again.

"What's your biggest weakness?"

After all that time, I expected him to come back with an answer that was insightful, maybe even poetic. Imagine my shock when instead, he looked me up and down, very slowly and very creepily, and said . . .

"You."

I told him he had five seconds to leave my office before I called the cops.

Other times I didn't even need the questions to help me weed people out. Their actions told me everything I needed to know.

About three questions into her interview, one applicant began rummaging around in the massive purse by her feet. I assumed she was searching for a copy of her résumé until a familiar aroma filled the air. Next thing I knew, she was holding a box of chicken nuggets. For a brief second I thought maybe she'd brought them to me as a gift, but apparently she was just hungry.

I fought to remain focused as she ate—no, *devoured*—her chicken nuggets right there in front of me, licking every finger and getting crumbs all over my once-spotless office floor. And just when I thought things couldn't possibly get any weirder, she asked if I had ranch dressing . . . which I grabbed from the office fridge and gave to her. (What else was I supposed to do?! Google hadn't prepared me for this.)

Chicken nugget girl got her dipping sauce, but she definitely *did not* get the job.

With every interview I conducted, I got better and better at knowing not just what I *wasn't* looking for in people, but also what I *was*. I couldn't put it into words, but within moments of meeting someone, I'd usually get a feeling in my gut about whether they were the kind of person I wanted representing Student Maid. And over the course of the interview, that feeling would almost always be validated. Applicants who didn't have the "it factor" didn't get the job. But even if someone *did* have "it," I hired them only if they also met all four requirements.

And then Jade came along.

Losing her didn't make me automatically throw my deal breakers out the window, but it gave me permission to bend them if I ever found myself in a similar situation again. Good thing, because a few months later, I met Andrew.

Andrew showed up to his interview even before I did. When I got back to the office after running an errand, he was there waiting patiently, ten minutes ahead of schedule.

Again, punctuality was a great sign, and the more I got to know him in the interview, the more I liked him. He *really* wanted a spot on the team, and he told me he wasn't afraid of even the messiest of messes. But there was a big problem: Andrew wasn't a student. He was out of school and had no plans to go back.

Just as with Jade, my gut told me Andrew had Student Maid written all over him. But not being a student seemed like an even bigger deal breaker than not having a car. I mean, *hello*, "student" is in our company name. Our clients expected only students in their homes. If this wasn't the be-all, end-all of nonnegotiables, then what was?

This time I let my gut win. I gave Andrew a job even though he didn't meet my number one requirement. I told him he could be our "student of life," and I'd be in touch soon to set up a time for him to come in and fill out paperwork. He was elated, and I knew I'd made the right choice because I was too.

Things got busy after that, and somehow I totally forgot to follow up with Andrew. A couple weeks after his interview, on what happened to be an unbelievably demanding day, Andrew called to check on his start date because he still hadn't heard from me. I apologized profusely for dropping the ball and explained that we were totally slammed— we had dozens of apartments to clean in a matter of hours, and we were quickly falling behind. Sensing I was overwhelmed, Andrew asked, "Anything I can do to help?"

I joked that he could help by starting his job that same day. Would you believe Andrew dropped everything and was there within the hour, ready to fill out his paperwork and go to town on some filthy apartments?

That confirmed it for me: gut > checklist.

—

Jade gave me permission to bend my rules, and Andrew was proof that I should.

He turned out to be *the* definition of a dream employee: He showed up early for work, constantly offered his ideas to improve the business, picked up extra shifts and covered for sick teammates, took initiative and left notes for his clients when they were running low on trash bags or dish detergent.

Never again did I let the boxes on my checklist become deal breakers. I realized I cared more about someone's work ethic and character than whether they had a car or were enrolled in school. (Our clients did too.) Even if someone's schedule wasn't ideal, I decided that if I felt strongly enough that they were Student Maid material, I would find a way to accommodate them. So from that point forward, if I met someone who made me feel the way Andrew had in his interview, I offered them a job without thinking twice. (After they passed a background check, of course.)

It proved to be a great strategy. Hiring based on my gut took Student Maid to another level. We rarely got new clients because of five-star reviews of our mopping abilities or the quality of our cleaning products. People usually hired us at the recommendation of an existing customer who'd raved about our hardworking, dependable students (and students of life). Our clients had so much trust and confidence in our team members that they soon asked for help beyond cleaning: We walked their dogs, tutored their children, house-sat while they went on vacation, decorated their homes for the holidays. One even asked us to usher her wedding. Another invited two of our recently engaged students to *move in* to her guest house and help take care of her home. (They did.) We became a full concierge service, and our office line rang so often that I had to upgrade our phone system.

All the new business we were getting was great, but I was way too busy to really appreciate it. Taking on additional customers meant that we needed to bring more students on board to keep up with the demand. And more students meant more interviews . . . which only *I* could do. It's not like I could teach someone else how to hire the way I did. That sense I got about an applicant when they walked in the door wasn't something I could articulate to anyone— not even to myself. It was just a feeling that I . . . felt. So even though I didn't have time to do all the interviewing, I made time. I crammed in interviews early in the morning before the office opened, in the evenings after we closed, between meetings and events, whenever I could find a free half hour. You might be thinking, *But Kristen, you taught people how to problem-solve, cheerlead, accept feedback— don't you think you could teach them how to—*

Nope.

Interviewing without me? Over my dead body. The stakes were just too high to take a chance on delegating something so critical to Student Maid's reputation.

Whenever a new client handed me a key to their house, I'd have this moment where I'd stop and think, *Wow. This is the key to their entire world.* They were allowing our students into the place where they lived, raised their children, cared for their pets, and kept precious and often irreplaceable objects. It was an act of trust on their part and a huge responsibility for me. I felt like I owed it to our customers to personally guarantee that each person who stepped foot in their home had my stamp of approval. Anyone representing Student Maid was an extension of me, and I was certain that the only person who could ever decide who should be an extension of me was . . . *me.*

That is, until the fateful night I discovered Tony Hsieh in the bookstore.

—

Rich was right when he told our group that reading was the key to becoming better leaders and building better companies.

After I finished *The Three Signs of a Miserable Job* and saw how much a single book impacted Student Maid and even my own leadership, I made reading a habit. Curling up with a paperback written by a successful CEO and sipping a cup of hot chai became my ideal Friday night. I even took a speed-reading class so I could get through several titles in one sitting. (The social life of a young entrepreneur is thrilling, let me tell you.)

I had my routine down to a science: I'd go to a local bookstore, take a stroll down the business aisle, grab something with an appealing cover, and sit in the adjoining coffee shop, searching every page for ideas that I could implement at Student Maid. I read all the usual suspects, from Dale Carnegie's *How to Win Friends and Influence People* to Jim Collins's *Good to Great*. I even started to read beyond the business aisle, picking up books by psychologists, politicians, and basketball coaches. If it was authored by someone who had experience working with people, I figured it could teach me something.

One typical weekend night, as I wandered up and down the aisles, a book called *Delivering Happiness* by Tony Hsieh caught my eye. The subtitle—*A Path to Profits, Passion, and Purpose*—is what jumped out at me. I wanted all three of those things (who doesn't?), so I started flipping through the pages, and within five minutes I knew this book and I were meant to be.

Hsieh and I were practically twins. He too was an entrepreneur from an early age and built his first "real" company in his early twenties. Two years later, he sold that company to Microsoft for $265 million. (So when I said we were twins, I meant up until that part.)

In 1999, as Hsieh was figuring out what to do with his millions, he came across an opportunity to invest in an online shoe company called shoesite.com. The founder hoped to turn it into the largest online shoe retailer in the industry, but he needed some major moola to make that happen. Long story short, Hsieh invested in the business, changed the name to the way more clever Zappos (a play on *zapatos*, the Spanish word for shoes), and a few years later became

CEO. From there, Hsieh completely transformed the company. Within ten years, Zappos went from just a few employees to more than a thousand, made a billion dollars (you read that right: *billion*), and managed to earn a spot on *Fortune*'s "Top 100 Companies to Work For" list seven years in a row.

Way to make a budding entrepreneur weak in the knees.

I darted to the register, found my usual booth in the coffee shop, and kicked my speed-reading skills into high gear to find out exactly how Hsieh did it. By the time I got to the end of the book, my highlighter had run out of ink. Everything about Hsieh's story was inspiring and everything about his company, incredible.

Delivering Happiness was a game changer for me. I had heard people talk about "company culture" plenty of times before that night, but no one had ever bothered to explain what it actually *was*. They'd just say that company X was "known for its great culture and people love working there," or that company Y was "losing people because the culture has gone downhill." I'd deduced that the better an organization's culture was, the happier its people would be. But what actually made a culture *good*?

My best guess was that it had to do with perks. The companies I'd read about and idolized usually had Ping-Pong tables in the lobby or beer on tap or nap rooms. I assumed that to keep our students happy, I had to give them that kind of stuff. So I spent whatever money we had left over each month (not very much) to offer what perks I could afford. I installed a smoothie bar when we moved into our new office (and by "installed" I mean I put two blenders on the kitchen counter and made it BYOF . . . bring your own fruit), and I hired a DJ to spin music in our office on Fridays (fun, but it made it hard to hear clients on the phone . . . or one another).

Thank heavens for Hsieh. He saved me from wasting any more of our precious resources on my misguided understanding of culture. He taught me that I already had everything I needed to keep my team happy without a smoothie bar, a DJ, or any other wacko idea I'm certain I would have come up with sooner or later. As it turns out, a company's culture isn't defined by its perks at all.

It's defined by its people. And it isn't something you can see, hear, or whip up in a blender. A company's culture is something you feel.

Hsieh wrote about the way it *felt* to walk through the doors of the Zappos headquarters. The way it *felt* to work there for eight hours. The way customers *felt* when they talked to employees over the phone. That feeling was the collective product of the individual attitudes, personalities, behaviors, and beliefs Zappos' employees brought to the company. That meant if Hsieh wanted the organization to have integrity, for example, he had to hire people with strong moral character. If he wanted Zappos to feel fun, he had to find people with a sense of humor who appreciated a good laugh. If the company hired the right people—people who "fit"—the feeling would stay intact.

But hire the wrong people—people who don't fit—and the opposite can happen. Hsieh knew this because he'd experienced it before. In his first company (the one he sold to Microsoft), a few bad apples joined the team during a growth phase, and they ended up spoiling the whole bunch. Soon, Hsieh didn't even want to come into work anymore. When he looked around, he saw people who were competitive, who pushed others down to boost themselves up. The company was growing like crazy and its potential was enormous, but Hsieh didn't care about that and neither did his best employees. He decided to sell it because it no longer felt like the business he used to love. Many people left with him for the same reason.

As I read, I had a revelation: The "special something" I felt in my gut when I met people I wanted on the team wasn't some random thing, and it wasn't the tacos I had for lunch either. As Hsieh had with Zappos, I had an innate understanding of how I wanted Student Maid to feel, and I was looking for people who would keep it feeling that way. That internal nudge telling me, *This one! This one! Hire this one!* was my gut knowing that person would be a good culture fit. And the reason I had been so selective about whom I let on the team—and why I was so reluctant to pass on the interviewing torch to anyone else—wasn't just a matter of customer trust; it was also a matter of preserving Student Maid's culture. Each person we let in the door would either keep our company feeling like the one we all loved or hurt it, maybe even turning it into a place we didn't recognize anymore.

When Hsieh got the chance to start over with Zappos, he made sure to protect the company's culture at all costs.

He knew the people he brought into the business would either make it or break it, so this time around he was super strict about who joined the team. But Zappos being as ginormous as it was, I knew Hsieh couldn't possibly be the only one on hiring duty. So how the heck did he manage to guard the cultural gate?

Allow me to introduce you to the *Commandments*.

They were as big and powerful as they sound.

The Commandments were Zappos' culture on paper—the ten core values that epitomized the fundamental beliefs and characteristics of all the people who worked in the company. They defined what made Zappos feel like *Zappos*.

To come up with them, Hsieh asked his employees to write down what the company meant to them. What traits did they admire in their teammates? What about working at Zappos made them proud? What did it feel like to walk in the door? He took everyone's responses and looked for underlying themes, and then came up with ten values that best represented what his employees believed the company stood for. Commandments like "Pursue Growth and Learning," "Create Fun and a Little Weirdness," and "Build a Positive Team and Family Spirit" make it easy to imagine how it must've felt to work at Zappos.

With the Commandments in place, Hsieh's employees were able to take over the hiring process so he could focus on bringing in $1.2 billion. The values became a guide that anyone on the team could use to assess whether an applicant belonged at Zappos. If the person shared the same beliefs and seemed like they would live the Commandments every day, they were hired. But if it didn't seem like they would—even if there was just a teeny, tiny ounce of doubt—the closest the applicant would ever get to Zappos would be buying shoes from the company's website.

Hiring was only the half of it, though. The Commandments also became the basis for deciding when it was time to let someone go. The Commandments were *truly* deal breakers, unlike the way I'd come to think about my hiring requirements. If anyone did anything that went against the values, no matter how long that person had been with the company, they were out. It sounds a bit harsh, but Hsieh believed it was the only way to protect the culture.

When I left the bookstore that Friday night, two things were abundantly clear: (1) I planned to stalk Tony Hsieh and Zappos forever, and (2) It was time to get us some Commandments of our own.

—

Here's the quick version of what happened next: I took a leaf out of Hsieh's book and asked our students to help me put our culture into words. I invited them to email me with their ideas (Andrew was the first to write to me—no surprise there), and within a couple days, I had more suggestions for our values than I knew what to do with.

Then Erin, Abby, and I took everyone's responses and narrowed them down to ten. We spent far too long coming up with super-cool names to match super-cool us, and I revealed the results at a super-dramatic team meeting. With "Eye of the Tiger" playing in the background from a pair of lousy, half-broken computer speakers, I unveiled the ten values that would guard our cultural gate and that we at Student Maid would hire by, fire by, live by, and one day most likely get tattooed on our bodies:

1. **Take your moral fiber.** We do what we say we're going to do, and we tell the truth.

2. **Roll with the punches.** When things don't go according to plan, we adapt.

3. **Jump through flaming hoops.** We don't just do what's expected; we go above and beyond, not only for our clients but especially for each other.

4. **Don't leave us hangin'.** We understand how our actions can affect others; we put the interests of the team before our own individual needs.

5. **Be classy, not sassy.** We show respect to one another, speak with discretion, and maintain a positive and uplifting attitude.

6. **Own it.** We take responsibility for our work and our decisions, and we care for Student Maid as if it were our own business.

7. **Unleash the creative dragon within.** We think outside the box to problem-solve and develop new ideas.

8. **Pay it forward.** We give back to our community, not because we have to but because we genuinely care and want to see the world become a better place.

9. **Speak now or forever hold your peace.** We maintain open communication with the entire Student Maid team, which means we voice all our concerns, questions, comments, criticism, and praise.

10. **Raise the roof.** We work at Student Maid because we love and believe in the company, so we put forth our best effort to help it grow and thrive.

You might be thinking you know what comes next. I'm about to tell you how our values helped us go from asking random interview questions found on Google to asking thoughtful ones that revealed whether someone fit our culture.

Not exactly.

Creating an interview process based on our values proved to be almost impossible. Erin, Abby, and I agreed that the values were our new deal breakers, and that even if an applicant had won the Olympic gold medal for rug vacuuming, we would hire them only if they appeared to embody the ten things we now deemed most important. That part was easy. We also agreed that I would shadow Erin and Abby as they did interviews until I became confident they could hire like me. That was easy too. But coming up with questions that revealed a person's integrity, creativity, or willingness to jump through flaming hoops? Not so easy.

We tried *everything.* We tested honesty by planting an expensive-looking piece of jewelry on the office floor to see whether applicants would take it or turn it in to us. We assessed creativity by handing someone a pencil and instructing them to come up with as many uses for it as they could in two minutes. We asked point-blank, "Are you a classy person? Are you adaptable?" (Amazingly, everyone answered the same: *Why yes, yes I am.*) We tried open-ended questions like "How would you define teamwork?" to see if their definition aligned with the way we defined "Don't leave us hangin'." We did everything except light hula hoops on fire to see who would actually "jump through flaming hoops."

I thought we'd be able to come up with values-based questions that would tell us beyond a shadow of a doubt if someone fit our culture, and I wasn't willing to completely let go of hiring until we did. But sometimes, even when applicants answered our questions well, my gut still told me they weren't a fit. The cool thing was, when I asked Erin and Abby what they thought, their guts told them the same.

I realized that in creating our values, I'd done what Hsieh did for his team: By writing down our culture on paper, I'd given Erin and Abby a guide to hiring like me. They knew our values. They lived them. They had helped come up with them, for crying out loud. All I had to do was give Erin and Abby permission to trust and follow their instincts in interviews, just as I had learned to do. If they did that, they would end up making the same decisions I would have. And for the most part, I was right: I passed the hiring torch to Erin and Abby, and nine times out of ten, we ended up with people I was proud to have representing Student Maid.

We continued our pursuit of the perfect questions, but we never found them. After several years of trying any and every question and test—and then a thousand more—we still have yet to discover anything that tells us with 100 percent certainty whether someone fits our culture. I've discovered that in an interview setting, applicants are typically on their best behavior. They will always give the answers they think we want to hear instead of the ones that reveal who they are. Whatever it takes to get the job.

Nowadays we don't have standard questions. We try to make our interviews flow like natural conversations, even though that's tough when applicants are nervous and trying to put their best foot forward. We start off by asking something like "So what's your story?" or "Tell me about your life," and then we sit back, listen, and let the candidate take the dialogue wherever they want it to go. Sometimes people try to nervously fill the silence and end up sabotaging themselves by ranting about how their last boss was a jerk or admitting to having a bad temper. In those cases, we get lucky; the applicants show their cards and weed themselves out. But even when they don't slip up, we usually discover more about someone this way than we ever did when we asked them to answer our questions.

Instead, we ask ourselves: *Would I feel comfortable if this person had a key to my house? Would I enjoy working with this person? Does this person remind me of our best team members, like Andrew? Or our worst, like Courtney?*

Just as Erin and Abby did, and I did before them, those who now oversee hiring trust their guts and their innate understanding of our culture to steer them in the right direction. It's important to note, though, that I've found this works *only* if the person doing the interviewing is the *best* example of a Student Maid team member and embodies all ten of the values.

Do they get it wrong? Yes. But so did I sometimes. Everyone does. There's no way to be certain that someone is the perfect fit for your culture just from an interview—you don't find that out until they get in the gate. That's why the interview is only the first of several checkpoints in the hiring process.

I figured out the next one when Erin quit.

—

The more people we hired who fit our culture, the more Student Maid blossomed.

One day Erin, Abby, and I were sitting around imagining what the future might hold for the company. It was always my dream—a dream I openly shared with them—to have a location in every college town, and now, for the first time, we were talking about the real possibility of opening a second branch. We all thought the time was right. The only question was where.

We wanted to pick a place close enough to drive to, just in case we ever needed to get there in a jiffy. We also knew we wanted to pick a town with a major university and lots of students looking for jobs. Of course, once we decided on a location, we'd need someone to lead it. I couldn't see myself moving out of Gainesville, and Abby wasn't keen on leaving either. That left Erin.

Erin was itching to move. Her longtime boyfriend lived in Tampa—a couple hours from Gainesville—and, understandably, she wanted to be closer to him. My brilliant idea was to open a spot in Tampa so Erin could be near him and stay with the company. With everyone seemingly on board, we made the trek to Tampa and started meeting with different apartment complexes to get a feel for the market. Because cleaning student apartments was how we'd made our mark on Gainesville, we thought we'd replicate that same strategy to get things off the ground in a new area. Why reinvent the wheel?

Our trip was even better than we'd hoped. One apartment group was ready to sign a contract right then and there, and several others wrote to us after we got back to Gainesville expressing serious interest in working together. So it was decided: Tampa, Florida, would be the future home of Student Maid's second location, and Erin would lead it.

Overcome with excitement, we made a list of all the things we'd need to do to bring the idea to fruition. Abby began skimming local ads for office space, and I got in touch with colleges in the area to tell them about our plans to hire their students. We hadn't signed any contracts yet because we wanted to wait until we'd saved a little more money before we opened the branch, but every day it felt like we were getting closer to pulling the trigger.

And then one night, Abby called me, completely distraught.

"Did you get Erin's email?" she asked, once she'd composed herself.

I jumped on my computer and felt my stomach drop. An email from Erin with "Notice" in the subject line was staring me in the face. In the message, Erin said she believed Student Maid had been a great opportunity for her, but she couldn't say that she had the same passion and excitement for it that I had, and she wasn't excited about managing our new location. She had decided it was time to move on, and she was putting in her two weeks' notice, effective immediately. She'd found another job in Tampa.

Abby was shocked, as was I. How could Erin just up and leave us like that? After everything? Setting aside my devastation and disappointment, I calmed Abby down the best I could. I told her we'd be just fine, even if it didn't feel that way in the moment, and told her that maybe this was happening for a reason. Both for us and for Erin.

If I'm being honest, I should have seen Erin's resignation coming from a mile away. All that time we were planning our debut in a new city, she never really got into it. Abby and I were searching for contracts in our free time. Abby and I were talking about the marketing plan over lunch. Abby and I brainstormed anytime we had a spare moment about how we could get involved on local campuses. Abby and I made the decision to open in Tampa—not Erin. It was never her dream. It was ours.

And in retrospect, it wasn't just Erin's indifference to opening a location in Tampa that should have been a tip-off. She and Abby were like night and day when it came to Student Maid: Erin would leave the office at 5:01 every day, while Abby would sometimes stay later than I did. I never heard from Erin on the weekends, but Abby would send me emails on Saturdays with her ideas to grow the business. Erin's facial expression didn't change when we talked about ten years down the road, but Abby's eyes lit up with excitement every time. If I needed help with something, I knew that of the two, Abby's hand would shoot up first. To Erin Student Maid was a job, but to Abby it was so much more.

Let it be known that Erin is an amazing person who did her job extremely well. She delivered on every promise. She never called out sick. She lived our values. She cared about our students and our customers. She was perfect on paper. Yet there was still a piece missing: She didn't want Student Maid as much as Student Maid wanted her.

Losing Erin was tough for us—even tougher considering she emailed her resignation after we had all worked so hard to get better at in-person confrontations. We had to pump the brakes on Tampa, and we lost a lot of time, energy, and resources that we could never recover. But I don't blame or resent Erin for that at all. In fact, I respect the fact that she gave us notice before we actually made the move and went through with it all. I also feel a bit guilty. Erin's decision to leave turned out to be the absolute best thing for her. I can't help but wonder whether she would have left Student Maid sooner if I had asked what she wanted instead of always thinking about what the company needed.

Erin's departure taught me to redefine "culture fit." Just because someone fit our culture didn't mean Student Maid was the right fit for them. We needed a way to help us determine before someone accepted a job whether they were as excited about joining the company as we were to have them on the team.

—

Abby and I knew that Erin wasn't the only member of the team who wasn't as invested in or as enthusiastic about Student Maid as we were.

We'd seen our fair share of two-week notices, sometimes within people's first couple months on the job. They'd tell us they hadn't expected the work would be so physically demanding or that they wanted to find a company with more opportunities for advancement. Every time we got resignations like these, we wondered whether we'd missed something. How could they not know this job would be physically demanding? Did they think we used Roombas? And *advancement*? Some of these people had been part of the company only a couple of weeks.

It was frustrating—and expensive—to invest so much time and energy into bringing someone on board only to lose them shortly afterward. But as Erin had shown me, it was selfish to make it all about Student Maid. How frustrating for someone to invest their time in the company and then come to the realization that it wasn't where they wanted to be. I wanted to avoid unnecessary heartache on both sides. So I started to think: How could we prevent mismatches from happening in the first place?

That's when Hsieh popped back into my mind. I remembered a passage from *Delivering Happiness* in which he mentions that, to weed out people who might not be fully invested in their jobs at Zappos, he offered all new hires $2,000 to quit. Hsieh figured that if someone took the money and walked, they were there just for a paycheck and not because they wanted to be a part of the company. He found it was actually cheaper to give someone $2,000 to quit than it was to invest time and resources in a person who was bound to leave the moment a better-paying opportunity came along.

When I first read this idea in Hsieh's book, I didn't think it was something we needed at Student Maid. But after what happened with Erin, I understood how smart it was.

I couldn't afford to pay anyone $2,000 to do anything. But even if I could have offered $20, I worried it would backfire and students who actually did want to be at Student Maid would take the money and run. When your hiring pool isn't made up of broke students who donate plasma to pay for their textbooks, I'm sure Hsieh's plan probably works. But we needed a way to identify new hires who really wanted to be a part of the team without forking over any cash—a way to make sure they knew exactly what they were getting themselves into with Student Maid and that they still wanted in.

That's how we came up with the Scoop, a document that

gave potential team members an inside look at what working at Student Maid and being part of our culture was really like. After a successful interview, we would email the Scoop to candidates we wanted to hire and request that, before they accepted a position with us, they read it in its entirety.

The Scoop had two sections. In the first, we included unedited comments from our current students about what they liked and disliked about working at Student Maid. If candidates thought a job where you could "learn your way around Gainesville" and "get paid while making lifelong friends" sounded awesome, then this would get them even more pumped about joining the team. If reading things from our students like "Pulling a hairball out of a vacuum sucks!" or "One time I found a dead hamster in a freezer" made them flinch, they might want to think twice about accepting a position with us.

The second section of the Scoop came from the leaders of the company, and we used it as an opportunity to tell potential hires what they could expect from us and what we would expect from them as a Student Maid team member.

We wrote about our focus on learning and growth and talked about how we encourage team members to think for themselves, problem-solve, grow from their mistakes, and self-manage. We explained that we challenge them to confront issues with their coworkers and leaders face-to-face using tools—like the FBI—that they learn in our required communication class. Our goal, we said, was for them to leave the company better leaders than they were when they came in, and in order for that to happen, they'd have to be invested in their personal growth as much as we were invested in it.

We were up-front about our not-so-competitive pay—due to our low margins and the resources we dedicated to things like our communication classes—and made it clear that we couldn't offer raises or traditional promotions for the same reason. We might give someone an opportunity to manage an apartment complex during our busy summer season or ask someone to plan our holiday party, but at the end of the day, every student would still have a sponge in their hand. Finally, we conveyed that because of the nature of our business, we couldn't guarantee anyone a certain number of hours each week. We promised to do our best when it came to their requests but warned that if they absolutely had to make a specific dollar amount each paycheck, Student Maid probably wasn't the best place for them.

The Scoop laid everything on the table. It prevented people from signing up for something that wasn't right for them and saved us from wasting anyone's time. It also reduced the number of students who resigned in the first few months of their employment. Not all, but it definitely made a difference. And whether someone accepted the position or declined, they were typically appreciative of our transparency.

My, how things had changed since I won back The 45.

I'd gone from never wanting anyone in my company to quit ever again to encouraging people to leave, no hard feelings, if they didn't feel it was the right place for them. We weren't afraid to show the real us—frozen dead hamsters and all—and we weren't afraid to lose people who didn't like what they saw. Tony Hsieh, I imagined, would be so proud of the culture we were protecting.

Except for that one time I did that one thing.

—

"Kristen?"

I looked up from my computer to see Morgan, one of our best team members, standing in the doorway to my office. "Can I talk to you for a sec?" she asked quietly. I nodded and waved her in.

"Um, so . . . ," she began. "So there's—there's someone . . ." She stopped and cleared her throat. "Um, can I . . . close the door?"

"Of course," I said. *Something's up.*

Morgan was usually one of our most confident and outspoken students, but her gaze kept shifting around the room, wandering from the shelves behind me to the wall, then down to her hands. Each time it seemed like she was going to say something, she'd stop and glance over her shoulder to make sure the door was still shut.

It was clear she needed to get something off her chest. Suddenly she looked right at me and said, "Someone is stealing from the company."

My jaw dropped. "What do you mean *stealing?*"

"She's exaggerating her hours on payroll and she's doing it on purpose," Morgan said in a rush. "The last time I worked with her she told me she adds something like five minutes or ten minutes here and there. She said you guys would never find out and she told me not to say anything, but I know it's against our values and, and . . ."

I could feel my blood boiling. We trusted our students to self-report their hours. Just thinking of someone violating that trust—and upsetting Morgan—made me want to kick a mop bucket.

"Morgan," I said, struggling to maintain my composure, "would you be comfortable telling me *who* is doing this?"

She leaned in close and whispered the person's name softly.

I was *livid*—but not surprised—when Morgan revealed the culprit. If anyone would do something like this, it'd be *her*.

I thanked Morgan for having the courage to come forward, and I promised her I'd take care of things right away.

You know how I screw up from time to time? This one's bad.

—

Fast-forward to about six months later.

A longtime client called the office wanting to know why her most recent cleaning cost $20 more than usual. She'd left a signed, blank check on her kitchen counter and asked the team to fill it out on her behalf, a common practice because of how much our clients trusted our students. Upon looking up the payment, we found that someone had written "$20 tip" on the check's memo line. But the client said she hadn't authorized a tip. *Who* on *earth* would do something like that?

You guessed it.

The same person Morgan had told me about months earlier—whom, by the way, I had never dealt with, even though I'd promised I would.

There's a lot wrong with this picture, I know. But let's cover the obvious thing first: How did a thief—we'll call her Jennifer—get a job at Student Maid to begin with? How did someone who so clearly did not "take her moral fiber" get past all our hiring checkpoints?

The short answer: We left our cultural gate unguarded.

The longer answer is slightly more complex.

Jennifer was hired during a period when, for the first time ever, we had clients on a waiting list. Thanks to the stellar students we'd been hiring, we'd earned a reputation for awesome service and for "jumping through flaming hoops." That meant clients were used to our dropping everything to accommodate them when they needed a cleaning ASAP, so it wasn't exactly a fun conversation when I got a "My mother-in-law is ringing the doorbell in three hours—*help!*" phone call and I had to tell them we could be there . . . in a *month*. If we didn't figure out a way to take care of wait-listed customers lickety-split, I feared they might ditch us and find another cleaning company.

So I put pressure on Abby—who, with Erin gone, now had a small team of students helping her with hiring—to get more team members on board as quickly as possible. With the wait list getting longer by the day, I instructed Abby and her team to think outside the box and do whatever it took to get people in houses . . . *fast*. We ended up hiring friends of friends without having them go through our standard hiring process. I assured myself that it was only temporary, that as soon as we got the wait list taken care of we'd go back to our normal practices. And that's how Jennifer ended up wearing the Student Maid uniform.

But it doesn't explain why she was allowed to *keep wearing it* after Morgan came forward. It might seem like I was reverting to my pre-Courtney ways and avoiding confrontation like the plague. But this time, I can assure you, I wasn't afraid of confrontation.

I was afraid of *Jennifer.*

Eva had warned me about "HR nightmares" when I was at the incubator and, unfortunately for me, Jennifer was their poster child. She was the kind of person you hope and pray will resign but never does. Jennifer exaggerated and told white lies more than the truth. She was unreliable and defensive, and she didn't get along well with other students. But whenever I tried to talk to her about these issues—and I had, plenty of times—Jennifer insinuated to her teammates that she would sue if she lost her job. Word, of course, always got back to me, just as she intended. I couldn't afford to risk a lawsuit and she knew it. So instead of letting her go, I let her manipulate me.

When Morgan told me about the payroll incident, I knew Jennifer would deny the accusations until she was blue in the face, and all I'd have would be Morgan's word against hers. But once I learned that she'd cheated a client, it was *on.* A copy of the check with Jennifer's handwriting on it, combined with Morgan's statement, offered indisputable proof that Jennifer was stealing from our clients as well as Student Maid.

Confronting Jennifer was like a scene from a movie. I ended up having to call the cops for backup. (HR nightmare is an understatement.) The worst part, though, was that Jennifer's toxicity was contagious. As I investigated the check situation, I discovered that in the six months since Morgan had come forward, Jennifer had been adding thirty or forty minutes to every shift on her time sheet. Then, to cover her tracks, she had conned other students into "enhancing" their hours to match hers. Multiply the added time by a few people over several months. . . . It was enough to make me sick. In the end, we lost money and destroyed the trust we'd worked so hard to build with one of our longtime clients. But what really killed me was the fact that Jennifer had convinced others to go against our values. Why did those students do it? Why hadn't they come forward and told me?

Better question: Why *would* they have come forward? Morgan had, and I had done nothing.

After everyone who was involved in the time-sheet scam was let go (yes, Jennifer too) and the dust settled, I invited Morgan to come along with me to a speech I was giving close to Gainesville. She hadn't been stopping by my office to catch up as much as she used to, and I wanted to make sure everything was okay.

During the drive, I thanked Morgan again for coming forward about Jennifer's theft, and I apologized to her for not taking action as I'd promised. Her response was brutally honest—and exactly what I needed to hear. Morgan told me she'd lost respect for me as a leader. Here I was, demanding that everyone commit to the values on Student Maid's wall, but when Morgan told me someone was violating them, I did nothing about it.

Morgan left the company shortly after that car ride. We parted on good terms. She told me she was leaving because she was ready for a new gig. But my gut told me that wasn't the real reason.

I thought back to Tony Hsieh and how he didn't want to come to work at his first company when he was surrounded by people who were destroying the culture he believed in. I think that's how it was for Morgan, who had to clean alongside Jennifer for hours at a time, knowing she was violating Student Maid's values, and had to see *me*, knowing I was letting Jennifer get away with it. Morgan probably felt like she didn't even know the company she used to love anymore, which was why she'd spoken up in the first place.

And that brings us to our last hiring checkpoint: our team members—and me. Together we are responsible for bringing our values to life.

I've found that what values *really* do is help the team members who are a good fit identify those who aren't by giving them something specific to look for. Our people then become stewards of our culture, helping us keep it intact by alerting us when we've got bad apples on our hands. But it's up to me as the leader—the head gatekeeper—to actually do something about it.

When Morgan told me about the theft, I should have immediately gotten rid of Jennifer, no matter how burdensome a potential lawsuit could be. Doing so would've shown Morgan that I meant what I said about living our values and protecting our culture, and it might have kept her at Student Maid a little while longer. But instead I let my fear of Jennifer keep me from doing the right thing. Morgan lost respect for me, and my inaction turned the values into nothing more than words on our wall.

With that hard lesson learned, I was determined to recommit to my role as the gatekeeper of Student Maid's culture. And that meant I had to stop ignoring the one component of the business that continually threatened to destroy it: move-out season.

—

The hiring spree that allowed Jennifer to get in wasn't the only time we let bad apples into our company. In fact, we left the gate wide open once a year, every year.

We'd been participating in move-out season ever since the summer of The 45. Thanks to our stunning, speedy finish after I won back the team, the apartment managers we worked with that first summer hired us again the following year. And just like my first Craigslist customer, they talked us up to all their property manager friends and told them they should work with us too.

We quickly became the most in-demand cleaning company for apartment complexes during move-out season. We were one of the only services in town that could actually get a high volume of units cleaned by the time new tenants showed up with their U-Hauls (and picky parents) on move-in day. So that meant we got contracts with new properties every year without even trying. Soon we found ourselves responsible for cleaning several thousand apartments each summer.

At first it was awesome. The entire season was only three weeks long, and it was our most profitable time of the year by far. We didn't *need* the money—we would've been able to keep our doors open without it—but having the extra influx of cash allowed us to grow much faster: It helped us move from the incubator to our office in record time (no, really: we beat an incubator record), and it allowed me to hire Erin and Abby full time. What was not to love?

Oh, you know, just . . . everything.

Months before the season even started, Abby and I would hole up in our conference room until the wee hours of the morning, trying to figure out how many hundreds of people we'd need to hire in order to clean several thousand apartments. That's hundreds of *totally new* team members, by the way: Our regular team of students would be busy taking care of our residential and commercial clients, so that meant we had to hire a separate, temporary team only for move-out season.

Which is where things started to go downhill.

With a small interviewing team and only a few weeks to recruit a workforce of hundreds, we had to lower our standards big-time. Forget checkpoints. Our "interviews" were a joke: We did group interviews, phone interviews, even *email interviews* so we could get through the greatest number of applicants in the shortest amount of time. All we focused on was volume. We didn't bother to send out the

Scoop because . . . why? They'd only be working with us for three weeks. Aside from a clear background check, we looked for only one thing: Does this person have a pulse?

How, after everything I'd learned, could I let this happen to Student Maid *every year*, you ask? Well, because really, I didn't see it as happening to Student Maid. In my mind, hiring for move-out season was like hiring people for a different company that existed only one month out of the year.

And what a month it was.

Each day of move-out season, we'd take these hundreds of people, split them up, and send them to clean at more than a dozen apartment complexes around town. Once they arrived at their assigned property, they'd be greeted by the best of our best: a select group of Student Maid superstars who had earned the dubious honor of becoming move-out-season team leaders. These leaders were our most dedicated, determined, high-spirited, and trustworthy people (think lots of Andrews). We put several of them in charge at each of the properties, where we would assign as many as a hundred move-out team members a day, depending on how many apartments we needed to clean. Then it was up to the team leaders to make sure every unit we were contracted to clean on that property was absolutely spotless before the property manager's white-glove inspection on move-in day.

Easier said than done.

The condition of the apartments ranged from not too bad to I-want-to-throw-up horrific: flea infestations, mildew, and huge garbage bags full of rotten trash left behind. And the turnaround time was so tight that to meet the property's deadline, we had to schedule teams to work around the clock.

But the team leaders' biggest challenge—even greater than roach-filled refrigerators and inch-thick dust—was managing the people assigned to them. We're not talking one or two bad apples who were newly hired. It was more like an entire orchard.

When the team leaders came by to inspect units or check on teams, it wasn't uncommon for them to find people sleeping, texting, fighting, goofing off, making *popcorn*, even watching movies on their phones. Every now and then they'd walk in and find no one at all. (Some people didn't even have the decency to quit in person like The 45.) Now, I'm being a little unfair—some of the people we hired for move-out season were great. Spectacular, even. But they were few and far between. Most of them didn't listen. They were rude and disrespectful—the opposite of classy. The opposite of *each* of our ten values. But even if we wanted them gone, we didn't have much of a choice. We needed every ounce of help we could get, even if that help came with an attitude. We did let people go who were truly awful, but we couldn't afford to cut every person who wasn't pulling their weight or we'd never get the work done.

That meant our team leaders had to pull all the weight, working throughout the night, picking up the slack so they could be on track for the next day. And as the season went on, things only got worse. More and more people on their teams quit, saying the work was just too hard. The ones who stayed developed even bigger attitudes the more tired they got. When I'd walk around the properties and hand out waters and pizza, it broke my heart to see the miserable looks on our team leaders' faces. These were the *best* people we had—the people who made Student Maid what it was—and they looked discouraged, fed up, and exhausted.

The second those three weeks were over, everyone—me included—wanted to quit Student Maid and take a yearlong vacation. Some of our best people started leaving every summer for internships or going back home to visit their families just so they wouldn't have to manage a property. I couldn't blame them: I wished I could leave too. So it wasn't just that I thought of Student Maid as a different company during move-out season—we actually *became* a different company. For most of the year, it was the place we knew and loved, but every summer it became a place we couldn't get away from fast enough.

But that would all change shortly after Morgan called me out for not committing to the values.

Summer was still months and months away, but I was sitting at our conference table as usual, waiting for our hiring team to assemble so we could have our first move-out-season meeting of the year. As I watched the team make their way into the room, I noticed the looks of dread on their faces. No one was looking forward to even *thinking* about the summer. As we talked about the properties we planned to work with and the number of people we'd need to bring on board, I happened to look over and glance at the wall where we displayed our values.

And it hit me: Why was I doing this? Why was I putting

my people through this again? I knew it was going to be hell. I knew it would bring the wrong people into the company. I knew that during move-out season our values would go out the window and our culture would take a nosedive. I knew our best team members would be absolutely miserable. Was it really worth it?

No. It wasn't.

As I sat there, I thought about what Morgan had said about losing respect for me after I let someone stay on the team who didn't fit our culture. By allowing move-out season to continue, wasn't I basically doing the same thing? Wasn't I allowing people to represent Student Maid who didn't embody our values *at all*? For years I'd let myself justify move-out season by saying it was just three weeks, the team we hired was only temporary, and it made us a bunch of extra money that we could reinvest in the company and use to help us grow. I also feared that if we stopped doing it, we'd make room for a big competitor to enter the market. But I had to think about our people and our culture and what something like move-out season did to both.

I introduced a radical idea to our team: What if we cut back on move-out season? Like, *majorly*. What if we committed to hiring for move-out season the way we would hire for our year-round team? Just because there was a demand for a high-volume cleaning service didn't mean we had to fill it, I argued. Not if it came at such a cost to our culture. We could take on less and hire *only* those who fit. We could do without the extra money.

Abby and the rest of the team looked at me like I had just

done a backflip in the middle of our conference room. It had never even occurred to any of them that we could choose *not* to do move-out season on the scale to which we were accustomed. Move-out season was a fact of life at Student Maid; we'd been doing it practically since day one.

So we talked. And talked. And talked. In the end, we decided our culture was more important than a super boost to our bottom line. The weight of the decision was huge, but once we'd made it, we felt so relieved. We went to the properties we'd been working with for years—far in advance—and told them about our decision to scale back and why we had made it. Though they weren't looking forward to a move-out season without their biggest, most reliable cleaning team, not one of the property managers faulted us for our choice, and in fact a few said they admired us for putting our people before our profits.

That year was like a freakin' vacation. For the first time, Student Maid felt like Student Maid all year long. We did significantly less work and lost out on a big revenue bump. But we hired carefully, and we ended up with a bunch of great new team members who stayed on our year-round team once the season was over.

Looking back now, it's amazing that it took me so long to change our approach to move-out season. But I'm not going to pretend I don't know why. It's hard to walk away from money on the table, especially when you're a cleaning company with small profit margins. But when I really sat down and thought about the intangible losses we incurred to make that profit, it was an easy choice.

As the gatekeeper of the culture, you have to protect it from everything that might damage it. Even if that means turning down a bunch of money.

—

A company is only as good as the people it hires. It's cliché as hell, but it's true.

I discovered early on that there's a difference between the rules that are meant to be broken and the ones you should never bend. It was Jade who taught me to look past my standard requirements. I now know that when we find great people, we should think about how we can accommodate them instead of watching them walk away. Some of the best people I've ever brought onto the team didn't meet a single requirement on my checklist.

And it was Tony Hsieh who taught me that values are the only real deal breaker there is. We've got to hire people whose character and beliefs align with the company's to keep the culture we love intact. But as I learned so painfully when Morgan came forward, we've also got to be willing to cut people loose when they go against the values, or they'll turn our company into one we don't recognize.

During periods of growth, companies are especially vulnerable. When money is up for grabs, it's hard to turn it down. But anytime we compromise our hiring practices to make more profit or serve more customers, we lose more than we gain.

5 ~~TURED~~ UPSIDE DOWN AND INSIDE OUT

"**C**hug, chug, chug, chug!"

Rowdy college students crowd into a living room, red Solo cups in hand, as Lil Wayne blasts through the speakers. The bass is so loud the pictures shake on the walls. Miraculously, the cops haven't shown up yet, but it's only a matter of time.

Empty beer cans litter the floor. The bathroom has been out of toilet paper for hours. The trash is overflowing, and the Jell-O shots are almost gone.

In the middle of the crowd, two of the drunkest people hold up the legs of a girl who is upside-down, grasping the top of a keg in both hands, and drinking Bud Light straight from the tap.

She gets some beer up her nose but keeps going, and the crowd goes wild.

She's *wasted*.

—

Keg stands are never pretty, but this one was particularly horrific for a few reasons:

Reason #1: It was my living room.

Reason #2: I was the girl.

Reason #3: The people holding my legs worked at Student Maid.

I know what you're thinking. After all I'd learned about leadership, how could I do something as stupid as *this*?

Well, after Erin left the company, things really took a turn. . . .

Totally kidding. This party went down a long time before that. I threw it in honor of my college graduation, right around the time I gave up a career in finance and chose to stick with Student Maid instead. Back then, I didn't understand that slurping Jell-O shots together was just *one* way to build relationships with the people on my team. I hadn't yet discovered I could also form bonds with them based on trust, vulnerability, empathy, and mutual respect, and that *that* kind of relationship would benefit me—and Student Maid—so much more than the kind that left everyone with nasty hangovers.

I've told you how I hired the right people to join my team, but now it's time for my favorite part of the story: how we went from holding up one another's legs to having one another's backs. How we actually *became* a team.

—

No matter how embarrassed I am by that keg stand, I can easily see how I ended up in such a compromising, upside-down position: I was the same age as many of our students when I hired them, and I saw them as friends more than as people who worked for me. I was a student running a business full of students. We went to the same pool parties and hung out at the same bars. We rooted for the same football team and hit up the same tailgates. A couple of us were even taking the same classes.

The fact that students had to pick up and drop off their cleaning supplies at my house back then didn't help either. Before the incubator days, it wasn't unusual for our students to come by on Saturday mornings and find me (and sometimes my roommates) sitting on the couch in pajamas, bed head and all. On payday, the students would line up in my driveway to get their checks, and sometimes they'd stay and chat with me on my front porch as we swayed back and forth in my rocking chairs. Even when they weren't working, they stopped by to say hi (and to raid my fridge). So inviting them to my graduation party was a no-brainer. That's how we rolled. Work together, play together.

Now, I'm not a moron. I realized it probably wasn't the most professional move to party *that* hard with the people whose paychecks I was signing. But it didn't bother me to blur the line between us. Let's not forget: At the time, I was in full cheerleader mode. And just as I was willing to turn a blind eye to missteps to keep people from walking out on me, I was willing to risk a little professional respect if hanging out and having fun together would make people love their jobs (and their boss). Pom-poms by day, beer pong by night.

My habit of attending wild parties with my team could have caused some real problems. Luckily, though, it didn't come to that. Instead, the more the business grew, the more Friday nights I spent in the bookstore and the less energy or inclination I had for house parties. Gradually, without giving it much thought, I started dropping out of the scene. But I didn't bow out completely until I introduced our core values and made a purposeful decision not to rage with my team again. The values on our wall reminded me that I had to be the example for our students, and that meant keeping it "classy, not sassy" at all times. (Keg stands are definitely *not* classy, no matter how gracefully you do them.) My new personal policy was no more parties, no more happy hour, no more gossip or asking everyone about their spring break plans. I was still the students' biggest fan, of course, but I figured I could cheer them on without being all up in their business. Now when I ran into team members between shifts at the office, I kept it professional, asking things like "What do you think about the new scrub brushes?" and congratulating them on their latest WOW Wall–worthy survey. The students who had been around the longest probably thought there was some *Freaky Friday* voodoo happening with how quickly fun-and-down-to-party Kristen became straitlaced-and-serious Kristen.

But that trusty gut of mine told me I still didn't have it quite right. I started to feel isolated, like I had to be a different person at work from who I really was. It felt disingenuous. I didn't really know the people who worked with me anymore, and they didn't really know the real me. I felt like I was in danger of taking a giant step back and becoming as distant from my team as I had been when I sat in that comfy armchair in the clubhouse. I never wanted to go back there. So what were my options? Should I just say "screw it" and throw another kegger so we could go back to how things used to be? Sounded good to me. I was pretty sure I still had some Jell-O in my pantry. . . .

But before I could get upside down again, my mentor, Rich, showed me another way.

—

My group meetings with Rich changed everything I thought I knew about being close to the people I worked with. And it started with being vulnerable.

When the group got together, we were supposed to share our deepest fears and challenges so others could provide perspective and support. But for the first couple meetings, I couldn't bring myself to open up. I hardly knew these people, and yet I was expected to tell them things I didn't even share with my family and closest friends. So I held back. I'd be losing sleep wondering how I was going to come up with enough cash to cover payroll or crying between business meetings over a falling-out with a friend, but when it was my turn to share, I'd talk about how I needed to find a different insurance agent or negotiate prices for cleaning supplies.

A cofounder of a music-streaming company was the one who finally gave me the courage to open up. Josh was part of Rich's group too, and his entire entrepreneurial journey had been a roller coaster from the get-go. He was essentially disrupting the industry by changing the way people shared music, and it seemed like nearly every month he was fighting another lawsuit from a major record label. Often he didn't know if he'd even be in business the next day. To people who didn't know him, Josh was as tough as nails. He never gave up, even in the face of endless setbacks. But I got to see a different side in our meetings. When Josh spoke, he never shied away from telling us how scared he was. He talked about how sometimes he wanted to give up and told us how the stress was affecting his personal relationships. None of that made him any less strong or admirable; in fact, it made us all admire him more.

Josh's vulnerability made it easier for the rest of us to let our guards down, me especially. Over time, we all became more comfortable talking about financial pressures, disgruntled employees, tough decisions, insecurities, and regrets. Our meetings weren't always heavy though. We also discussed our dreams: the impact we wanted to make, the people we intended to marry, the things we wanted to cross off our bucket lists. I'd tell you more, but I'm sworn to secrecy. (What's said in the room *stays in the room*.) Our meetings became our refuge, the place we could completely be ourselves and say how we felt without being judged.

Rich knew what a difference it can make to have the support of others who understand your struggles. That's actually the reason he started our group: He didn't want anyone to feel the meaning of the saying "It's lonely at the top." Although he'd never belonged to a group like ours, his relationship with his business partner, Darin, offered him the same kind of refuge. Rich and Darin hadn't planned to cultivate a deep, meaningful friendship, but that's what slowly happened over time. When they first started their business, the two would often drive to see customers and suppliers, traveling for days at a time. Hours in the car led to hours of conversation. They'd start out talking about what was and wasn't going well in the company and their goals for the future, but with so much time on the road and only so much business to discuss, their conversations often got personal. Just like our group, they shared things with each other that they hadn't told anyone else. Their understanding of each other grew, and they became closer. They made their relationship a priority, and in time, their investment in each other paid off. Now, more than twenty-four years later, Rich believes that their bond is what allowed their company to weather storms of all kinds and come out on top. He compares it to a family: The more the parents focus on their marriage, the more stable things are for their children during life's ups and downs.

I was inspired. While I didn't have a cofounder, I did have Abby. And in many ways I saw her as my business partner. She didn't have any financial or legal stake in Student Maid, but her heart was in it just as much as mine was. Even more so after Erin left and it became the two of us.

Naturally, I was a lot closer to Abby than I was to the students because we worked together every day. We knew each other well enough that she could sense when I was stressed just by my facial expression, and I could tell when she was hungry based on her tone of voice. It became obvious to her when I needed a caffeine boost, and it was obvious to me when she needed alone time.

But I gleaned from my group meetings with Rich that Abby and I had barely scratched the surface of our relationship. If we were supposed to be the parents of our company that meant we better start working on our marriage.

—

Unlike Rich and Darin, Abby and I didn't have a business-related reason to be out of the office together for an extended period of time. So that meant I got to play travel agent.

Our very first road trip, or "retreat," as we eventually called them, was *really* bare-bones. While I wanted to fly us to a swanky boutique hotel on an exotic island in paradise, all I could afford was a two-night stay in a double-queen, nonsmoking room at a Marriott two hours away. I kept the itinerary simple: a lot of informal sharing, reflecting, brainstorming, and goal setting between eating takeout and relaxing. On the business side of things, we came up with some great ideas on that trip, including a monthly book review where we'd each read a different business book and share what we'd learned over breakfast. But the best part of the trip was that it gave us a chance to bond on a personal level in a way we couldn't at the office. We talked in depth about our families, friends, and relationships, and, just as Rich had experienced, we felt closer when we returned home.

Abby and I continued to go on retreats at least once a year, escaping for four, sometimes five days at a time.

Thanks to Student Maid's growth and to Groupon deals, we took trips to Miami, Las Vegas, and Sedona. Our retreats became our treasured time together. We always started with a really honest conversation about the year, focusing more on what we wanted to change than on what seemed to be going well. We reviewed our annual budget and made game-changing decisions for the business. We learned we had similar fears about being responsible for a team of students that was growing larger every day.

At the end of every retreat, we were both more excited about the company and where we were headed. And with every trip, our friendship grew deeper. The more we learned about each other, the more we trusted each other. And the better we were able to take care of each other personally and professionally.

Once, Abby came into work looking distracted and on edge, which was very unlike her. She told me quietly that she'd just learned that a close family member would have to undergo emergency surgery with a high risk of complications. Knowing Abby—who pushes through no matter what's going on in her life—I knew she'd ask for the bare minimum amount of time off. I encouraged her to take off as many days as she needed, starting right away.

When the day of the surgery came, I was so anxious I could hardly concentrate on my work. In a way, it felt like *my* family member was in that operating room. Abby finally called me later that afternoon, and I could hear the relief in her voice: Everything had gone smoothly. I cried tears of joy and I'm pretty sure Abby was crying too. Later she told me how much my support meant during what was one of the scariest times in her life.

Being there for Abby felt right. But what if I hadn't known what she was going through? What if she hadn't felt comfortable enough opening up to me and hadn't gotten the time off she needed to be with her family?

I wanted us to be able to support our team members through their hardships, just as I'd done for Abby. But that meant Abby and I had to know more about our people and what they were up against in the world outside the office. How could we help them feel comfortable sharing those aspects of their lives with us? No way I could take all of them on a retreat: Student Maid was doing well, but not *that* well.

During our next trip together, Abby and I brainstormed ways we could get to know our students better. Our winning idea was that at least once a week we would each spend one-on-one time with a different team member outside the office. Getting away from work during our retreats had helped put us in a different frame of mind, which is what we wanted to do for our students, so that (we hoped) they'd be more willing to open up. We'd go to a coffee shop, restaurant, frozen yogurt place—pretty much anywhere except a keg party.

At first our conversations felt awkward and a bit forced, which is not surprising, considering most of us millennials "friend" people on social media more often than we make new connections in real life: Four in ten of us say we interact more with our phones than friends and family. The more Abby and I met with students, though, the more comfortable they got talking to us. We learned about their hobbies, saw pictures of their pets, and heard stories about favorite aunts and grandfathers. Sometimes they vented about classes they were struggling with or their fear of not finding jobs after graduation. Eventually we reached the point I'd been hoping to get to: They started to become more forthcoming about personal situations that affected them at work.

A few days after I had coffee with a student named Charlotte, she found herself in a tough spot: Her apartment lease was ending, but she wasn't allowed to move into her new place until the next week. In the meantime, she had nowhere to go. Her friends had all left for the summer, and she couldn't afford to stay in a hotel. Charlotte confided in me that she was planning to sleep in her car, and as soon as I heard that, I told her, "Absolutely not, Charlotte! You are going to stay at my house." She just stared at me for a second, shocked, and then told me she couldn't possibly accept. But I insisted. Charlotte stayed with me for three days, and then she moved into her apartment. All was well.

When I tell people that story, they look at me with as much surprise as Charlotte did: "You let *an employee* stay in your *home*?" they say.

Yeah, I did. It might seem inappropriate to a lot of people, but to me it was the right thing to do. I cared about her more than I cared about keeping some kind of arbitrary distance between us just because I happened to hold the highest position on the totem pole. When she graduated,

Charlotte told me she'd never forget how I helped her out when she had nowhere else to turn.

I was starting to understand that my responsibility as a leader wasn't to party with my people, and it wasn't to shut them out either. I was there to support them every chance I got. And the better I got to know them, the more I came to truly care about them.

Every team member was important to me, but there were a few who made me wish that the end of their tenure with Student Maid wasn't predetermined by their graduation date.

Maybe, I thought, they'd be interested in staying with Student Maid even after they graduated. Maybe they'd be excited to help Abby and me grow the company. Couldn't hurt to ask, right?

So I did. And lucky for me, they said yes.

—

These wonderful people I hired full time became what we call our "leadership team," and in the couple years following Erin's departure from Student Maid, that team went from just Abby and me to a group of four of us. Then six. Then seven. Then ten. We could barely fit around our conference table. One more and I'd be sitting on someone's lap.

We all knew one another, considering we'd been working at the same company together for quite some time, but this was our first time working directly together, and we weren't anywhere as close as I felt we needed to be. My relationship with each person and their relationships with one another had to be strong. To make the best decisions for Student Maid and for our students, we had to be in sync. Retreats had helped Abby and me become closer, so I added annual retreats for the whole leadership team to the budget with the same goal in mind. And as the leaders of our new leaders, Abby and I kept up with our Groupon rendezvous as well.

For our group retreats, we'd rent a big house somewhere within driving distance (except for the one time we got a great deal on a cruise), and we'd lounge on sofas and balconies as we evaluated the year behind us. Taking everyone away from their desks encouraged us not only to put the past year at work in perspective but also to interact in ways we'd never had a chance to before. We learned who was a really good dancer (and who wasn't), who had serious skills in the kitchen (and who burned toast), who rose with the sun (and who loved the snooze button), and who was really good at roasting me (all of them were).

I was surprised by how intimate the retreats could be, even with so many of us there. As I had experienced with Abby, conversations about work naturally gave way to more personal conversations and often became therapeutic discussions. We always came away from our trips better friends and closer teammates and with a greater understanding and appreciation of one another. When we went back to business as usual, our sense of camaraderie permeated from inside our office all the way to the parking lot. We ate lunch together most days, and we sometimes even challenged one another to impromptu Nerf gunfights. (I'm screaming "millennial" right now, aren't I?) If someone had enough work to keep them in the office late on a Friday, we all pitched in until it was done so they didn't have to stay alone.

As I had anticipated they would, our group retreats also did a lot of good for the business. We used the time to set new goals for the year ahead and to come up with new projects and ideas, as well as to decide who should be responsible for implementing each one. We'd always return from our trips filled with a renewed excitement about our work and an eagerness to dive into our projects right away.

That energy among us naturally trickled down to our students. They'd bump into us before a shift and see how energized we were to be at work, and it made them more excited to be there too. Our revenue kept climbing. New clients kept signing up. But this time we were growing *and* keeping our culture intact. It made me want to revisit the idea of opening a second location. I thought we were ready.

Ever since we had put the kibosh on our Tampa branch, I'd been keeping my eyes peeled for our next chance. But I didn't have to look very hard: One day a promising opportunity just fell into my lap.

I got a call from an executive at a large resort in Pensacola Beach, Florida. She'd heard about Student Maid from a former team member of ours, and when her resort needed a new cleaning service for its high-end condos, she thought of us. The executive wanted to know if we'd consider opening a location there. If so, we'd have to move quickly: They needed us to be up and running before the start of their busy season, which was only six months away.

Pensacola was a little (a lot) farther from Gainesville than Tampa was—a grand total of 350 miles away. There weren't any direct flights from one city to the other. But we were talking *hundreds* and *hundreds* of condos. Even though I wanted to tell the executive yes on the phone, I knew two things needed to happen first: We had to meet these people, and we had to find someone willing to run Student Maid number two. (Can somebody say growth? Old Kristen would have definitely skipped these steps and said yes immediately.)

Just as with Tampa, neither Abby nor I wanted to move, and franchising was out of the question. Plenty of people had expressed interest in owning a location, but I knew strangers wouldn't be able to replicate our culture, and I couldn't do that to the Student Maid name. To get it right, the leader of the branch would have to be a current team member or alum, someone who had firsthand experience with Student Maid, someone who knew what it *felt* like to be a part of Student Maid. One member of our leadership team in particular stood out to me.

Rachel, who was actually *from* Pensacola, had been cleaning houses with us for about a year. Just months before I got the call from the executive, she'd graduated from UF with a degree in journalism, but so far she hadn't had much luck finding work in her field. Well, those newspaper fools didn't know what they were missing. Not only was Rachel loyal, dedicated, and Ms. Positivity, she was a fantastic writer. While a cleaning company certainly wasn't the place for the future editor of the *New York Times* to be honing her skills, I knew how much of an asset Rachel was, so I offered her a position on the leadership team until she found her next gig. Rachel wrote our monthly newsletter, edited our website copy, and helped me start a blog.

By most accounts, Rachel was in no way qualified to run a business. But neither was anyone else on our team. Only twenty-two, she barely had any job experience outside Student Maid. But she lived our values, and she was the kind of person who I knew could cultivate relationships to build a team like the one we had in Gainesville. With time and training, I was certain she could figure out the rest.

When I first approached her about the job, she was excited, but she didn't quite believe I was serious. Her initial response was "Kristen, you are aware my degree is in journalism, right? Not business?" (And your point is . . . ?)

Not too long after that, I drove with Rachel and Abby to Pensacola for what we thought was a meet-and-greet with the person who had called me. *Wrong.* When we arrived at the resort, we were led to a conference room where ten members of the resort's executive team—including the CEO—were waiting for us. It was like déjà vu. I felt exactly how I did when I blindly entered a bidding war for the apartment complexes our very first summer. This time, though, I had backup.

The executive team didn't go easy on us: One of the first questions they asked was why they should trust such a young company. I tried to ignore my trembling hands as I feigned confidence and suggested they call the hundreds of clients we'd had over the years and ask *them* why they should hire Student Maid. After some back-and-forth, everyone was all smiles.

While the opportunity seemed promising, Rachel, Abby, and I knew we had to do our due diligence to be sure. We researched the area, visited local colleges, and met with the chamber of commerce. All looked good. Finding students to hire wouldn't be a problem, and neither would expanding beyond the resort to clean residential and commercial spaces. Rachel returned to Pensacola a few weeks later to do a trial cleaning for the resort and brought someone from our team with her to help. The executives who inspected their work said it knocked their socks off. They were in. And so were we.

To get Rachel ready for the big move, I knew I couldn't go all "fail and figure it out yourself" on her just yet. Obviously that was going to happen, but I at least had to give her a sturdy foundation to stand on. Rachel worked alongside Abby and me to get hands-on experience in HR, sales, marketing, and operations. Throughout the process, I encouraged her to ask every question and voice every concern she had. I remember one night before she moved she asked, "What happens if I lose a receipt?" As long as you don't lose forty-five people, I told her, you're good.

Even though I was sure Rachel was up to the job, I still worried about her trying to juggle all parts of the business on her own. (Been there, done that, got the T-shirt.) She needed someone she could count on no matter what, who would shoulder some of the responsibility and be there to commiserate and celebrate with her. She needed an Abby.

Rachel's college roommate, whom we'll call Sara (her real name is Rachael, but we have a hard enough time keeping them straight, so I'll make it easier for you), was from Pensacola as well and hadn't yet found work in her field either. Rachel asked her if she was interested in being her wing woman, and happily, she said yes.

A few months later, we were packing a U-Haul with cleaning supplies, vacuums, and love, and Rachel was headed back to her hometown, ready for an adventure. As she pulled out of the parking lot, the whole leadership team cheering and waving, I shouted that I'd be in Pensacola to see her as often as I could and that I'd call her every day. I'm not sure she heard me over the roar of the moving truck's engine. Good thing, because my promises died faster than the bugs on the truck's windshield.

—

Student Maid was going through a growth spurt like none we'd experienced before.

While Rachel and Sara were interviewing and hiring students in Pensacola, back in Gainesville the clients kept on coming. More contracts. More students. More leadership team members. More. More. *More.*

And then, as if we weren't busy enough, we decided, *Hey! Let's become software developers!* (Didn't see that one coming, did ya?)

Google Calendar had been our go-to tool for keeping track of client appointments for years, but our needs were rapidly outgrowing its limited capabilities. We tried dozens of fancy software programs but couldn't find one that had all the features we wanted. I went to a few of my more tech-savvy friends to see if they knew of anything out there I'd missed, and I got a surprising suggestion from one of them: Josh, my friend from Rich's group with the music-streaming business, said if the software didn't exist, we should just go into business together and create our own. He figured if Student Maid needed it, chances were other cleaning companies did too. Josh and I had become extremely close friends over the years, and we actually made a pinkie promise one night to start another company together someday. We had a lot of the same views on culture and business and thought it'd be fun to see what we could create. This was our chance: We partnered with two developers, applied for a technology grant from the state, and with our input and their coding skills, we built a custom scheduling app for Student Maid that we also began selling to the cleaning industry.

At about the same time, as if we didn't have enough on our plates, we learned the building that housed Student Maid's office had been purchased and would be bulldozed to make way for a new development. The space was much too small for us now anyway, so it turned out to be a good thing. And thankfully, we had enough time before they tore it down to find a new location and remodel it into our dream office: a brightly lit, beautifully decorated, huge, open space. I wanted to do everything possible to create a space that brought people together and helped foster relationships. We built a coffee bar, a kitchen where we could cook meals, and a living room area where our students could sit on big, comfy couches and catch up before their shifts. We had a place where they could study, as well as a library filled with all the books that had helped me along my journey as a leader. We even had *windows* (a big deal for us). Our new space was the headquarters I'd always wanted for Student Maid. Not because it was big or because we had flat screens, but because our team members *wanted* to hang out before and after their shifts. To them it felt like a second home, a place where they felt comfortable being themselves and talking openly. Some would even come in on their days off to hang out and study.

I planned for it to be my second home too. But shortly after we moved in, my speaking career really took off. My former business professors had been asking me to share my story of founding Student Maid with their classes for years, and now the word had spread to other college campuses. I was being invited to talk to students all over the country about leadership and entrepreneurship and to teach them the things we taught our own team members at Student Maid, like the importance of committing to values and how to confront their peers. Student Maid's success with keeping our team members engaged as they cleaned toilets also sparked the interest of companies and organizations beyond the college market. I went from rarely leaving Gainesville to giving out-of-town speeches eight or nine times a month. I saw airports more than my office and hotel rooms more than my bed. Forget about visits or daily phone calls to Pensacola. I was lucky if I could find time to see our team in Gainesville at this point.

This new arrangement was far from ideal, but between setting up Pensacola, developing the app, and remodeling our office, we had made some big financial commitments. I wasn't willing to put us through the hell of move-out season again and watch our culture suffer just to make a buck, so I decided that my speaking would contribute to paying the bills until our newest ventures could sustain themselves. But even though I loved speaking, it was a lot of pressure on me. After about a year of being a road warrior, I started to feel something in me change.

When I first opened Student Maid, I would spring out of bed in the morning before my alarm rang, and most days I'd stay at the office working until after midnight. But now waking up felt like a chore, no matter how much sleep I got. I knew that by the time my feet hit the ground I'd already be behind on my work. I just couldn't keep up. Who wants to wake up to *that*? When I'd fly back to Gainesville, I'd have only a couple days before I'd have to pack up and leave again. So instead of chitchatting at the office, I'd make a beeline for my desk and close the door behind me so that I could get a ton of work done. The leadership team could sense I was stressed, so they interrupted me only if they absolutely had to, and when they did, I multitasked, typing emails as I promised them I was "listening" and told them to go ahead and tell me whatever they needed to tell me. They understood; they were overwhelmed too. I wasn't the only one with a growing collection of folders, printouts, sticky notes, and empty Starbucks cups on my desk. And I wasn't the only one keeping my door shut.

I knew our growing to-do lists and sudden unavailability affected our students, and it killed me. The leadership team set the tone of the office, so when we didn't go out of our way to talk to anyone, our students didn't either. Plus, with that fancy app we built, everything students needed to know was on their phones, minimizing the need for conversation. We didn't have time for weekly coffee chats. Our dream office was dead on arrival. The hallways were quiet. The common areas we'd built to bring people together were mostly empty. Instead of eating lunch in our dining area, people ate lunch at their desks.

Now I know the easy solution would have been to take a step back and stop taking on projects or cut back on a few. But in the moment, I couldn't see a solution. I couldn't even spare the brainpower it would take to come up with one—I needed every neuron focused on making sure I boarded the right planes. I just . . . kept going. What's that physics rule? What's in motion stays in motion?

All these projects were started with the best intentions. I was looking for other ways to grow and bring in revenue so we never had to loathe our summers again. But even though we had all the right people on board, we'd suddenly gone from Nerf gunfights in the hallway to "DO NOT DISTURB" signs on our doors. Who *were* we?

—

Two of our interns were responsible for solving our identity crisis—completely by accident.

For a project for one of their classes at UF, they came up

with the idea of monthly lunch-and-learns, where the audience (our leadership team) would bring a bag lunch, and the interns would find speakers to talk to us about managing money, working efficiently, setting goals, and more. The point was that we'd have ongoing professional development brought to our doorstep.

So guess who they approached to be the first speaker?

Me. For my own company. (How convenient.)

Even though I had a million and one things to do, I agreed to it. So now I had to come up with a way to keep us busy for two hours.

Well, as it turned out, that part was easy: I had just returned from taking the "Listen Like a Leader" class at Barry-Wehmiller University—where I learned all about those handy FBIs and effective communication—so I decided to use the time to talk about the class. We started in the conference room, eating our homemade lunches, completely overwhelmed at the thought of being away from our desks for two hours. But by the end, the energy in the room felt as high as it did after a weekend-long retreat. I'm not sure what did it—my recap of the content of the course, being in the same room together for the first time in a long time, or maybe some combination of the two—but as we wrapped up for the day, everyone was upbeat and talking . . . and *laughing*. Before we left, someone asked when we could do something like this again. I was thinking the same thing. (Bravo, interns.)

After the lunch-and-learn, the office seemed different. The last few days I was in town before my next speech, I worked with my door open, and I noticed everyone else did too. We were all working harder to connect with one another. If I was in the middle of something when someone needed me, I asked if I could finish what I was working on before I talked to them so I could be present instead of distracted. Instead of emailing Abby about our latest business challenge, I went to her office to talk it through. I even gave my team a recognition FBI, thanking them for giving up their afternoon for the lunch-and-learn and telling them how grateful it made me feel to have the time to reconnect with them. The leadership team started having lunch together again in the common area, greeting students as they came in to get their supplies. The students stuck around after their shifts and chatted with me too, asking about my latest speeches and travels. By the time I left town, our office was back to feeling like the dream office it was meant to be.

As I got back on a plane and left for another round of speeches, I felt sad to leave. Reuniting with the team had made me realize how much I missed them. We had been so focused on managing our rapid growth that we hadn't been focusing on one another. Being in hotel rooms alone, away from them, was making me depressed. I was reminded that I loved my company because of the people in it, and no technology in the world could substitute for the real thing. I could only imagine how isolated from the leadership team Rachel and Sara felt in Pensacola.

Somehow we'd taken our relationships for granted, but the lunch-and-learn showed me that it required very little effort to bring the team back together. Even two hours made the biggest difference. I wished we could make it a regular thing. Actually, scratch that. I *had* to make it a regular thing. We'd done a good job establishing our relationship as a team, but if we weren't making an effort to maintain that relationship, what good was it? Devoting time to team bonding just once a year at our retreats wasn't going to cut it. I knew I could count on being in town at least once a month, so I decided to use that time for team-building meet-ups in our office. That's how our monthly workshops were born—and they changed *everything.*

Every month, I'd put together an agenda aimed at strengthening our bond as a leadership team, and for two to three days, we'd meet for a solid *six* hours each day in our conference room. I asked Rachel and Sara to make the drive to Gainesville when it was feasible for them to be away, but if they couldn't, they'd tune in via videoconferencing. I knew taking people away from their work for that long right in the middle of the week was a lot to ask (a few people thought I'd made a typo when I sent out the first agenda), but this was important. So important, in fact, that I went to great lengths to protect the time we had together, just as I would go to the ends of the earth to protect our culture. I hired a student to answer the phones and take messages for the team and insisted that everyone put away their cell phones and laptops unless we needed them for the workshop. They weren't happy about it initially, but I gave them a few breaks throughout the day to check their email and play catch-up.

As for the content of the workshops, I had plenty of material to choose from because I did things like this to help executive teams of other organizations all the time. (How ironic. Kind of like the hairdresser who does everyone's hair but their own.) The first few workshops focused mainly on self-discovery. We took online assessments that gave us greater insight as to what our natural strengths were, learned whether we were more extroverted or introverted, took tests that defined our personality and behavior, you name it.

We thought we knew ourselves before we took these assessments, but they uncovered all kinds of talents, behaviors, and quirks we weren't aware of. Some of us, including me, learned we were more emotional thinkers, while others on the team relied more on logic and didn't let their emotions affect their decision making at all. Some of us discovered we got energy from being around people, which is why we loved to eat lunch together in the common area, while others were drained by being around people for too long and sometimes needed to be alone to recharge. Some had trouble executing, while others excelled at it. A few were very adaptable, while others naturally resisted change.

The more we understood ourselves, I figured, the more we would understand the way we interacted with others. And the more we understood about one another, the better we could work together. And sure enough, that's what happened: I learned, for example, that not everyone loved brainstorming as a group as much as I do, which explained why some people stayed silent and wrote down their ideas instead of shouting them out during meetings. So the next time I called a brainstorming session, I made attendance optional, provided that those who chose not to show emailed me their ideas instead. The result was a list of ideas ten times as long, as well as gratitude from the thoughtful introverts of the team who appreciated that I had changed up my style so they could contribute their ideas in the way that worked best for them.

We all looked forward to our workshops each month, although it was overwhelming for everyone to consistently block out so much time. We would walk in stressed, thinking about all the work piling up, but within an hour we'd all be centered and back in sync again; we remembered that out of anything we did each month, this was the most important of all. The social aspect was nice too. Eventually I started hosting our workshops at my house instead of the conference room for the same reason we went somewhere outside of Gainesville for our retreats: Getting out of the office, even if we were still in the same city, allowed us to turn off our "work" mode and spend time together just being ourselves. We'd curl up on my couches, and people were more inclined to linger afterward and catch up. Soon we added an optional postworkshop homemade dinner and a movie to the official agenda. (So much less dangerous than alcohol-induced acrobatics.)

With every workshop, our team felt more like a family . . . a feeling that got even stronger when I hired my mom.

Yes. My *mom*.

—

Never in a million years did I think my own mother would someday be one of the most valuable members of our leadership team.

I don't know if I ever officially offered her a job. It just sort of . . . happened. Both my parents helped me a lot with my business as it grew. My dad, as you might recall, provided legal advice (which I actually *listen* to now), and my mom would come to Gainesville for several weeks during our busy summer season to help in whatever capacity we needed: picking up supplies, unlocking apartments, cleaning out vacuums, washing cleaning rags—you name it, she would do it, no questions asked. (Can you say Mom of the Year?)

After my younger sister, Lauren, moved to New York City for a job, my mom was experiencing her fair share of empty-nest syndrome, so she filled her time by making the hour-and-a-half drive from her house and helping us in the office more and more. She didn't want to move to Gainesville because she had my dad to consider, but she started staying at my house and coming into the office a few days—sometimes more—every month. And then, suddenly, she was on the leadership team. Like, for real. I came into the office one day and everyone was calling her Bob, which is *not* her name (it's Maureen). When I asked her why, she told me she had given herself a new title. Turns out "Bob" stands for "boss of boss." (Ha! I'll let her keep thinking she is.)

Seeing my mom in the office took me a while to get used to, but I was surprised at how much I loved working with her. The rest of the team loved working with her too. Sure, we had to bring her up to speed on a few things (like, we send emails instead of memos, and no, we don't own a fax machine), but aside from technology challenges, she fit right in. She thought so too: no cross-country road trips in an RV or African safaris for Bob's golden years. Being the Student Maid jane-of-all-trades, she told us, had become her dream job. But just because she was family didn't mean I gave her special treatment. She attended our monthly workshops along with the rest of the leadership team and took all the same assessments. We learned she's an extrovert, she's task oriented, and she's motivated by checking things off her list—no surprises there for me. She was my *mom*. I lived with her for eighteen years. I figured there wasn't anything I could learn about her that I didn't already know.

I couldn't have been more wrong.

—

Through my speaking, I ended up at a conference in Dallas put on by The Container Store. Shortly after I got off the stage, Robert Jordan, a Southwest Airlines executive, gave a talk. He opened with a story about a meeting that completely transformed the relationships within his team, so you know I was all ears.

Jordan had recently become head of the airline's commercial group and had inherited a team of about a dozen highly qualified people. Normally, Jordan said, he got straight to business during meetings, but this group was pretty disjointed. They seemed to be having trouble relating to one another and working as a team. So he kicked off this particular meeting with a story. Not just any story, but a deeply personal one. He told his team that when he was a kid, both his parents suffered from severe mental illness and were often unable to take care of the family. As a result, Jordan became the adult at a young age, assuming the care of his two younger brothers. He learned to take charge and get things done because he didn't have a choice. He told his team he wanted them to know these things to shed light on why he could seem controlling at times and why his natural tendency was to micromanage. He wasn't trying to make excuses for himself. He just wanted to give them some context for his behavior.

He gave the group a minute to absorb what he had said, and then he told them he was giving them the floor. He asked each person in the room to share something from their childhood that had shaped them. One team member who had a reputation for being slow to make decisions and resolve disagreements explained that he had been raised in a household with conflict and explosive outbursts, which was why he now tended to avoid confrontation at all costs. One by one, each person told their story—happy, sad, and everything in between. By the end of that meeting, their perceptions of one another had completely changed, and it helped them come together as a team.

Much like the rest of the room, I was blown away by Jordan's willingness to share something so deeply personal about himself and his past. His candidness reminded me of Josh's in our meetings with Rich. It inspired me to open up to my leadership team in a way I hadn't before and to see if they would be willing to do the same. We were functioning pretty well as a team already, but this, I thought, could bring us to a whole new level of understanding.

I opened our next leadership team workshop the same way Jordan had opened his meeting.

"There's something I want to share with you about my life," I began.

I looked around at the mildly concerned faces staring back at me. Definitely not how they were expecting me to start the workshop.

"I . . . So, when . . . When I, um . . ." *This is harder than I thought.* I forced myself to keep talking and ignore my shaking voice. *Here goes nothing.*

I took a deep breath, and then I told them this story.

When I was in elementary school, my dad left his job as the county attorney. Some newly elected officials who didn't like that he worked on sustainable development and historic and environmental preservation forced him to resign. The whole ordeal was very public, and the media covered it for what seemed like forever to a ten-year-old kid. I didn't quite understand what was going on, but I knew that the actions of the people who opposed my dad were unfair.

My dad opened his own practice, and he continued to work on these public-policy issues for other governments and citizen groups. He was incredibly busy, and he had to work out of our house until he established an office of his own, which meant his files had to come with him. Boxes and boxes of research and planning documents ended up in my bedroom, stacked along one of the walls, because my bedroom had the most empty space of any room in the house. I *hated* sharing my room with the boxes. It was a daily reminder of what had happened to my dad. I put big white sheets over them to make the boxes go away.

As time went on and my dad's practice got busier and busier, more boxes and legal papers piled up, and soon they were in several rooms of our house. My dad didn't want them there, of course; he just had no other place to put them for the time being. The clutter, combined with the stress of such a big change, took a toll on my mom. Some days she seemed so sad. The house felt messy and out of control, and in hindsight maybe that's how she felt about our lives back then. So that's when I started cleaning. Every single day I'd come home from school and clean and organize everything I possibly could in an almost obsessive way. I hoped it would help my mom see past the boxes and files and be happy again.

My dad eventually got an office and everything was fine after that, but I've never let go of my need to have an organized, mess-free space. It's probably why cleaning came to mind first when I wanted those jeans.

As I wrapped up, I said, "I've never really shared how this affected me with anyone before." Not even Bob.

Then I asked the silent room, "Would any of you like to tell us something about your life?"

Everyone was suddenly very interested in looking at anything *but* me. Or one another. I knew I'd made them uncomfortable—but that was my intention.

"I'd like to share something," Bob spoke up. I can always count on Bob. I expected her to talk about something I already knew, but instead she told a story I had never heard before.

"Once, when I was thirteen or fourteen, my family went out to eat," she began. "This was a real treat for us because my parents didn't have a lot of money and I was one of five kids. My dad worked really hard, but our budget was tight. I wanted to pitch in, so when I was old enough, I got a job and gave my paychecks to my parents."

My eyebrows shot up. She gave her *paychecks* to them? I knew times had been hard when she was growing up, but not *that* hard.

"We carefully chose a restaurant with a sign that advertised that it was a 'nice, clean place with good food,'" Bob continued, "but that's not what we found inside. The restrooms were filthy. The food wasn't good. I watched my dad pay for what to us was an expensive meal at the time, and I was *furious*. In my mind, the restaurant was cheating my dad out of his hard-earned money. I told him we should demand a refund. So my dad handed me the receipt and told me I could write the company.

"As soon as we got home, I sent the company an angry letter and told them exactly how I felt about the injustice of it all. To my surprise, a few weeks later, I got a letter of apology from them with a full refund. And that was the first time I became aware that speaking up when something is unfair can actually do some good. This was also the first time I stood up for someone and fought for them, and it made me want to do it even more."

I couldn't believe what I was hearing, but it made so

much sense: After Bob had started working with us, I had been amazed to learn that she was insanely good at (and passionate about) collecting overdue money. Whenever someone said they would pay us and didn't or a store refused to give us a refund when we bought something faulty, a different side of her would come out. She had some sort of magic powers that got people to settle their dues. And she didn't only go to bat for our company. She also helped our team members with their financial maltreatments: When a student's apartment complex refused to return her security deposit, Bob helped her get it back. She did things like that for people all the time. And no *wonder*.

As my mom ended her story, I felt a rush of guilt. I started thinking about when I was in high school and there was a lot of tension between us. Most was caused by your average teenage angst, but the rest of it revolved around money. When I turned sixteen, she used to tell me where to gas up my car, even though I was spending my own money. She would make me drive across town for gas that was two cents cheaper per gallon. I'd argue with her, lovely bratty teenager that I was, and tell her to stop controlling me. At the grocery store, she would hold up a line at the checkout counter just so she could find a coupon at the bottom of her purse that would save her twenty cents, and it humiliated my sister and me. We'd poke fun at her, but my mom didn't find it funny.

Now here I was, looking at my mom, realizing that nearly every argument we'd had about my gas tank could have been prevented—or at least toned down—had I understood this part of her life. I felt terrible for making fun of her with my sister. Clipping coupons wasn't something to laugh at: It was a habit she'd formed out of necessity in the days when her and her family's lives depended on being frugal.

That day in the conference room, what I learned about my mom forever changed my relationship with her. I never argued with her about money again. I see her as a completely different person now—for what she's been through in her life and the way in which she helps people. Bob is my favorite person on this planet and has become my favorite person I've ever hired. I'm so thankful I've gotten to know her for the woman she is—and not just my mom—but I never thought that Student Maid would be the place it'd happen. And as I'd suspected, it wasn't just Bob whom I saw differently after that workshop. I learned so much about each one of the members on the leadership team.

The next person to share talked about being raised in a military family where her dad would be gone for six months out of the year. In his absence, she watched as her mom became tough and strong as the only leader of the household, which shaped her view of what a leader should be. Now, she said, her own leadership style tended to follow her mom's example, and that's why she might unintentionally step on people's toes. Another shared that as the older sister in her family, she was expected to set the example for her brother and follow the rules, and because of that, she felt she could never voice her opinions. So now she found it hard to speak up. The last person to share talked about how he had moved around so much as a kid that he had learned not to get too attached to anyone or anything, which was why he was very adaptable. But, he said, some people might mistake him for being detached or uncaring.

Sharing my story about the boxes with my team was harder for me than speaking to an auditorium full of thousands of strangers. Digging up a heavy emotion from my childhood—well, that took more courage than I was willing to admit. But by telling that story, I'd made it "safe" for my mom to come forward with a powerful story of her own and for the others to follow suit. That's when I realized that my job as the leader wasn't just to support others; it was also to be vulnerable. If I wanted us to be open with one another, I had to be open myself.

Following that workshop, I made a point of sharing more about my life with the team. And not just about the past; I talked about what was happening in my day-to-day: my fears, my struggles, my sleep deprivation.

I remember one workshop where I was a mess. That month I had nearly double the speeches I usually had, and I was so behind at work that I was having chest pains. Normally I would've held it together and told myself I had to suck it up and be the strong leader. But this time I broke down to my team as I would have with a close friend. I will never forget when one person put her hand on my shoulder as I cried, telling me all would be okay and that she and the others were there to help. No one looked at me like I was doing something wrong or shameful. No one doubted my abilities as a leader. Instead they asked what they could do for me. We spent the rest of the workshop divvying up as many of my responsibilities as possible so they could help me tackle them. I'd never felt more grateful to have such a close-knit, understanding team. And I realized that sometimes leaders need support too.

To some people, the way we interact as a team seems way too touchy-feely, and my openness is TMI. When I talk about vulnerability and the relationship work we do at Student Maid, I always get at least one or two eye rolls. Some people say, "That crying crap doesn't belong in the workplace," or they say we "sound like a bunch of hippies." One time a guy in the audience asked me sarcastically, "So you're saying if someone's dog dies, I'm just supposed to sit and cry with them?"

First of all, *yes*, you heartless monster.

Okay, I didn't actually say that. But I wish I had. What I really told him is that being vulnerable and open and allowing people to *feel* at work isn't about crying with someone. It's about understanding what they're going through so you can work better together.

Every now and then, just leaning over to the person next to you and asking, "How are you doing?" can make a huge difference. What if they're going through a divorce? Or a loved one just got diagnosed with cancer? Or they've suffered a devastating loss? What if they're just having one of those weeks where everything that can go wrong has?

We can't expect people to just leave their feelings, worries, and hardships at the door and then pick them up again when they leave work. They're bringing that baggage with them. And they're likely to be too distracted, upset, and unmotivated to do their jobs if there's something bothering them. Knowing what's going on in a person's life and being aware of their mental state at work doesn't just allow you to offer them support. It also allows you as a leader to do what you need to do to make sure your organization runs smoothly, which might mean reassigning someone's to-do list so that it still gets done, as my team did for me. But when you don't know what's happening, you can't help, the work doesn't get done, and no one wins.

—

Everyone on our leadership team understands the benefit of investing time and energy in one another and in our students. Today, when we see our students in the office, we make a point of putting down our work to spend time chatting with them. In fact, we actually pay our students to hang out for fifteen minutes both before and after their shifts specifically for the purpose of building relationships. If we aren't around to chat, they can use the time to get to know their coworkers better. Our students could easily keep their supplies in their cars and meet their partners in the parking lot to carpool, rarely setting foot inside our doors. But we require them to come inside because we've learned that if we want to encourage close bonds within our team, we have to be intentional about it and make time for people to cultivate them. It's expensive to pay everyone in our company for an extra thirty minutes each time they work, but to us, it's money well spent.

When it comes to actually forming a relationship, we don't just expect that our students know how to do it. In the same workshop where we teach them about FBIs, we also teach them tools for building connections with people in and outside of work. We even have them take the same self-assessments we took as a leadership team to help them better understand themselves and how they relate to others.

One of the biggest things we teach our students in that workshop is that text and email are terrible ways to communicate about *anything* that matters. At the Barry-Wehmiller course, I learned that only 10 percent of communication is actually made up of the words that we speak. The remaining 90 percent is composed of things like our body language and nonverbal cues—nodding our heads, looking someone in the eye and smiling. (And no, emojis do *not* count toward that 90 percent.) Even virtual face-to-face conversations (via things like Skype and FaceTime) don't really cut it because we're missing the body language. Sure, video chatting is better than text or talking on the phone, but the only way we can truly give 100 percent is by being together in person.

At Student Maid we have an informal policy that text messages and emails should be used only for quick, informational exchanges like "What time should I meet you at the client's house?" or "I left oven cleaner out for you." Anything significant, like giving FBIs, needs to be done in person.

I try to set the example. These days I don't even have an office in our dream headquarters anymore, and I'm still out of town more than I'm in town. But when I'm there, I work from my laptop in our common area, where I can strike up conversations with students passing through. I seize every opportunity to look our students in the eye, to be vulnerable with them, to empathize, to ask them about their happy times and their sad times, and to support them when they need it. Even a thirty-second exchange can make a difference and mean the world to someone. One student told me that during his first week, I stopped what I was doing and made a point to walk up to him and say hi. Years later, he told me, he still remembers and appreciates that.

When we bring our humanity to work, so do our people.

—

A few years ago, a man called our office looking for a cleaning service for his elderly mother, Ms. Byron. He told us she needed help maintaining her house but warned us that she had become very grumpy with age and was extremely particular, so we'd need to send someone with thick skin.

We had the perfect person for the job: Meghan, one of the most upbeat, outgoing, and compassionate students on our team. She had been with the company for a few years and was studying to be an elementary school teacher. She lit up any room she entered, making it impossible *not* to smile around her.

Meghan began cleaning Ms. Byron's house about once a month by herself. Working solo is unusual for our students, but Ms. Byron's son wasn't sure his mother would tolerate more than one other person in the house with her at a time, and Meghan said she was okay doing it alone. Before long, Ms. Byron's son called to request that we increase the frequency of cleanings; whatever Meghan was doing was working, he said. Not only was his mom's house spotless, but Ms. Byron's spirits were lifting. He was starting to enjoy being around her again.

Meghan started cleaning every other week, and then Ms. Byron's son bumped up the frequency to weekly. Ms. Byron had grown to love Meghan, and the connection went both ways: Meghan always looked forward to cleaning Ms. Byron's house, and she told us that each time she was there, she struck up a conversation with Ms. Byron to learn more about her life. Even though they were far apart in age, Meghan and Ms. Byron were forming a close friendship.

After about a year, Ms. Byron's health unexpectedly took a bad turn. Her son called us to cancel services, as Ms. Byron was being placed in hospice care. When we broke the news to Meghan, she was devastated.

A couple days later, Abby was in the office working late when the phone rang. It was Ms. Byron's son.

"You aren't going to believe this," he said to Abby. "My mom is on her deathbed, and when I asked what her one wish in the world was right now, she asked for Meghan."

"She wants Meghan, right now?" Abby asked, wanting to make sure she understood him correctly.

Yes, he said. That was all Ms. Byron wanted.

Sadly, Meghan didn't make it to Ms. Byron's bedside before she passed. She was crushed; Ms. Byron meant so much to her. But Meghan had no idea just how much she meant to

Ms. Byron. Her son told Meghan that he had never seen his mom get as close to anyone as she had with her. He even asked if Meghan could help the family pack up her things and share the stories Ms. Byron had told her that no one else had heard. To thank Meghan, the family gave her Ms. Byron's favorite Oriental rug, and to this day she keeps it in her house to remind her of their special bond.

Every time I share that story in a speech, I choke up. I mean, on what planet does someone ask their cleaning person to be with them in their last moments? *That* is the power of creating relationships. *That* is the kind of bond that forms when you encourage people to open up and support one another on an emotional level. *That* is what happens when you create a place where it's okay for people to bring feelings to work.

—

Holding someone up while they chug beer upside down builds one kind of trust. But letting down your guard to admit when you're struggling builds a much better, much deeper kind. In one, you get nothing but a hangover. In the other, you walk away feeling accepted and supported.

When we bring people together and build a strong bond among them, we make them feel taken care of. Like they're a part of a family. It has a ripple effect, and those who feel taken care of take care of the people around them in return. Just as Meghan did for Ms. Byron.

6 ~~HOLDING~~ THE LINE

I remember where I was when I got the call.

I had just arrived in Michigan for a much-needed vacation. The table was set for Sunday dinner, and I was surrounded by friends I hadn't seen in a while. As we sat down to eat, I could hear my phone buzzing in the other room. I ignored it in favor of catching up with the people around me. But it buzzed again. And again.

Fearing there was some sort of emergency, I excused myself from the table to go check it. I was surprised to see Sam's name on the screen—Sam was Josh's partner in the music-streaming business. Since Josh and I had started making software together, I'd gotten to know Sam pretty well, but not so well that I'd expect to get a call from him on a Sunday night.

I picked up the phone. "Hey, Sam, what's up?"

"Kristen." His voice trembled. "Josh passed away."

My heart clenched in my chest.

"Wh . . . what?" I said softly.

Sam couldn't speak through his sobs, which was proof enough that I'd heard him correctly.

I suddenly felt dizzy, like the room was spinning around

me. I made my way over to the couch and sat down. How could this be real? Josh was only twenty-eight. He was healthy and full of life. I had just seen him a few days ago.

"Sam . . . what happened?"

All Sam knew—all anyone knew—was that Josh died in his sleep. We comforted each other as best we could over the phone, and then Sam asked if I would share the news with Rich and the other members of our group. He knew how close we all were. By this point, we'd been meeting every month for more than four years.

After we hung up, I just sat there. Numb. Dreading the conversations I knew were coming.

I called Rich, along with everyone else in our group. Then I got in touch with the software developers whom Josh and I had hired together, as well as Abby, whom I asked to notify the rest of our leadership team. Josh had spent so much time in our office working on our app that he had become an honorary member of our Student Maid family. The calls were just as bad as I thought they'd be. It was awful to be the bearer of unbearable news—to hear the same response of shock and disbelief and sadness over and over.

It had been only an hour, but it felt like days since I'd left my friends in the dining room. When I told them what happened, they wrapped their arms around me and offered their condolences. Then I headed upstairs and started packing. I didn't know what to do other than get on the next flight to Gainesville.

As soon as I landed the following morning, I headed to the Student Maid office to be with the team. I was walking through our parking lot when I got a call from the local newspaper. They wanted me to comment on Josh's sudden passing. That, strangely enough, is what finally made his death feel real. I stood on the sidewalk, eyes filling with tears as I told the reporter how much I felt for Josh's family and his employees. He was the kind of leader we would all be so lucky to have: mentally tough and courageous but filled with compassion, generosity, and humility.

As I hung up, grief washed over me. Crying turned to ugly crying, which turned to barely breathing. I looked around me and thought, *Josh was here just a few weeks ago.* He parked in the same parking lot. He walked on the same sidewalk.

The days leading up to Josh's funeral were some of my bleakest. Rich thought it'd be good to have a group meeting so that we could help one another cope. We went around the room and talked about how much of an impact Josh had on each of us, as if the chair he usually sat in weren't empty.

Even now we aren't sure how Josh died. The only cause of death was death. But I take comfort in knowing that a part of Josh will live on in me—and everyone who knew him. He didn't have a lot of time on this earth, but he sure made it count.

I promised Josh I'd do the same.

—

Fortunately, not all good-byes are as tragic and unexpected as Josh's passing.

Yes, some farewells are heart-wrenching, but there are other kinds too. The bittersweet ones. The ones that are blessings. The ones you see coming. And the ones you have to face before you can move forward.

I've never been good at any kind of ending. Especially at Student Maid. But Josh's death serves as a constant reminder to me that sometimes you have to say good-bye, even when you don't want to. Of course, there's a big difference between the death of a friend and the departure of a teammate; between letting go because you have no choice and choosing to let go because it's the right thing to do; between leaving words unsaid and knowing you did all you could; between the losses that aren't your fault and the ones that are.

The end of any relationship is scary, and when it ends, it usually hurts. But the more good-byes you say, the easier it is to distinguish between the people you should hold onto as tightly as you can, while you can, and the ones you should set free.

Here's how it happened for me.

—

Kayla joined the team during one of our earliest move-out seasons, back when it was just Abby and me running the place. The leadership team wasn't even a twinkle in our eye.

When I met Kayla, I was handing out cleaning assignments at an apartment complex. The property manager had approached me about adding another unit to our list, and as she described it in all its smelly, horrific detail, I silently prepared to say thanks, but no thanks. But before I could get a word out, a voice from behind me chimed in.

"I'll do it."

What the . . . ? I turned around and there she was. Light brown hair. Green eyes. Infectious smile. I'll never forget it. Her name was Kayla.

She told me it was her third day on the job, and I told her she really, *really* didn't want to clean that apartment. But Kayla insisted she didn't mind, so I decided to walk her through the unit to let her see it for herself and, hopefully, rescind her offer.

As soon as we opened the front door, I thought I was going to hurl. I couldn't even go in.

Not Kayla. She walked right inside, took a look around, and gave me a big thumbs-up from the window.

"Are you *sure*, Kayla?" I shouted with my T-shirt over my nose, desperately trying to escape the appalling stench— and I was *outside*.

Two thumbs-up. And she was smiling.

That nasty apartment was the first of many Kayla volunteered to clean. She never complained; she never gave up. And whenever she was done cleaning, the place was immaculate. In all my years at Student Maid, I'd never seen anyone clean like her.

When the summer ended, it was a no-brainer to offer Kayla the chance to stay on our team year-round cleaning homes and offices instead of only apartments. She gladly accepted the invitation, and our clients quickly fell in love with her. They began requesting Kayla more than any of our other students, and they even told their friends to hire Student Maid so they could experience her superhuman cleaning powers for themselves.

Despite her talent, however, Kayla—like all of us—had her faults. Chief among them was that she couldn't be on time to save her life. At first it was only a couple minutes here and there, but then a couple turned to ten, and ten to twenty.

Each time Kayla realized she'd overslept or was running behind, she would call and apologize profusely. She never meant to do it, she said, and she always took full responsibility. I simply gave her a shit sandwich (these were pre-FBI days) and asked her to do better in the future. Our clients tended to be flexible, especially if it meant getting Kayla as their cleaner, and she had so many other wonderful qualities, I didn't think her lateness was a huge deal. Plus, as I learned, she had much more important things to worry about.

As I got to know Kayla better in one-on-one coffee chats, she confided in me that things had been rocky for her ever since she could remember. She came from a dysfunctional family. She grew up around substance abuse and was raised in a home with emotional and physical abuse. My heart broke for her.

Determined to make a good life for herself, Kayla saved until she could move out on her own. She enrolled herself in community college and took as many credits as she could afford. But her family situation was toxic, and even though she'd moved out, it was still affecting her. With hardly any support system, I feared that Kayla might drop out of school and end up back in her family's grip, so it was my impulse to take her under my wing. I gave her leadership books to read and encouraged her to stick with her classes. The time I devoted to her seemed to be making a difference. She always told me she didn't know what she'd do if Student Maid wasn't in her life. So I resolved to keep Student Maid in it—which meant forgiving her shortcomings.

But Abby disagreed with my plan.

Abby cared about Kayla and felt sorry about what she was going through in her life, but she was adamant that we couldn't keep looking past Kayla's tardiness just because she had personal hardships. She said that being on time was one of Kayla's responsibilities as a team member, and there were plenty of other students in our company who had struggles outside of work but still managed to be punctual. Each time Kayla was late, her cleaning partners had to pick up the slack, which wasn't fair to them, Abby argued. To make matters worse, Kayla wasn't improving, even after I'd asked her many times to do better. Abby felt it was time to draw the line. If we let Kayla stay on the team, she said, we'd be setting a bad precedent for the rest of our students and sending the message that everyone could be late all the time and still keep their jobs.

Abby wanted to show Kayla the door. I wanted to keep her safe inside.

Had it not been for all those trips and retreats that Abby and I took together to strengthen the bond between us, I'm not sure how we would have weathered the Kayla days.

Every time Kayla was late and I kept her on the team, Abby and I argued. We hung up on each other. We stayed silent.

I'd promised Abby that she was my partner in everything we did. That we would make decisions together and that her opinions would carry the same weight as my own.

And I'd promised myself that I would support, take care of, believe in, and fight for every person in my company. Always and forever, no matter what. It's what I had to do for Kayla and what I would've done for Abby if the situation had been reversed.

The tighter I held on to Kayla, the more I worried I'd lose the relationship I'd worked so hard to cultivate with Abby. But if I let go of Kayla just to keep the peace, I wouldn't be able to live with myself.

If you're thinking this is usually the part of the story when someone wearing a cape flies in to teach me the thing that saves the day, you're right.

It's a bird!

It's a plane!

It's Marty Schaffel!

—

Marty is my business soul mate.

We met by chance at a local start-up competition, where participants had three days to form teams and start companies completely from scratch. At the end, the teams would present their new start-ups to a panel of judges for feedback and a chance to win funding. I just happened to swing by on the last day to serve as a volunteer and help teams prepare their pitches. Marty, on the other hand, was there to be a judge. He started an audiovisual company in 1979 that now has more than two thousand employees and brings in $750 million per year in sales. Safe to say he knows a thing or two about business.

While I was working with one of the teams, Marty stopped by and introduced himself. Just as Rich and I had, Marty and I connected instantly. I remember one of the first questions he asked me was if I had my own definition of "leadership" yet. I told him I was still working on it, but that I was interested in hearing his.

Marty told me he believed there was a big difference between managers and leaders. Managers, he explained, give orders, not ownership. Leaders, on the other hand, ask themselves, *How do I get this person to do what I want them to do and make sure they feel good about doing it?* (I thanked him for saving me the time of coming up with my own definition; I'd just use his.) This set off a several-hours-long discussion about culture, which led to Marty asking me to sit on the competition's judging panel with him, which led to Marty becoming one of my most treasured mentors.

As we got to know each other better, Marty and I were amazed to learn how similarly we thought. We had the same views about what it meant to care for our people, and we talked constantly about how to get the people in our companies even more engaged. Just for fun, he'd give me these outrageous scenarios (often from his own experience) and ask me how I'd handle them. Once, for example, he presented me with this dilemma: "A private school student voluntarily turns himself in for breaking the rules and smoking pot at school. Do you expel him or let him stay?" Easy: I said I'd let the student stay because he was honest, and that's the behavior I'd want to encourage. Marty grinned at me and said, "You took the words right out of my mouth, kid."

Marty lives a few hours from Gainesville, so whenever I'm in his neck of the woods, I take the opportunity to visit with him and his family. During one of my visits, as Marty and I caught up over wine by the pool, I turned the tables and gave him a scenario of my own.

The situation with Kayla had been going on for months, and it hadn't improved. If anything, it was getting worse. She was showing up late to work even more frequently now, and Abby and I still fiercely disagreed about whether to keep her on the team. I wanted to know how Marty would handle it.

"What would you do?" I asked. He sat quietly for a few moments, contemplating my predicament.

"I've been there," he finally said, "and it's a hard spot to be in."

He asked me if I wanted to hear about a similar situation that had cropped up in his company some years back. Different scenario but same dilemma. His Kayla was a guy named Pete.

I was all ears.

"Pete was an outside salesperson of mine and had a territory that required a lot of travel and driving," Marty began. "One month he made an entry on an expense report that favored him. I discovered it about a month later and was totally taken aback. I would have never expected something like this from Pete. So I confronted him and told him how devastated and disappointed I was. I told him this required immediate termination—and I was in tears as I did this. Pete was extremely apologetic and begged for a second chance. But everyone else in the company felt there could be no leeway. If anything required termination, this was it. No exceptions. But something told me this situation was different. Pete had some personal hardships that had caused him to do this—he was struggling financially. I knew he was a good person who cared deeply about the company. The black and white needed to melt into gray. So I offered Pete a second chance—a *zero-tolerance*, final-warning second chance. Everyone disagreed with my choice, but then Pete went on to have a very successful career at my company. Never again did he do anything to violate my trust in him."

Marty had done what he felt was right, even though it went against what everyone else thought he should do. And in the end, it worked out for Pete and for the company. I told him that I knew it would be the same in Kayla's case. But the tension it was creating in my relationship with Abby worried me. I couldn't help but think that maybe I was doing something wrong.

"Let me ask you something," Marty continued. "Do Kayla's strengths outweigh her weaknesses?"

"Absolutely," I said immediately. "Without question."

They really did: Kayla was an excellent cleaner. She cared about the company. Her heart was in the right place.

And she might have been late, but she always took responsibility for it and made up for it by picking up extra shifts.

"Then the answer is simple," Marty replied. "You can't let her go." I took the biggest sigh of relief.

Marty could tell that Kayla was incredibly special to me, given that I was willing to fight for her at the cost of my relationship with Abby. And he told me that because her strengths outweighed her weaknesses, he agreed that fighting for her was the right course of action. But, he cautioned, I had to be careful. If Kayla's tardiness continued, at some point it would become an even bigger problem that could end up hurting my relationship with Abby beyond repair, which would likely cause Student Maid's culture to suffer.

Marty challenged me to help Kayla break her habit and learn to be on time. If I could get her to do that, problem solved. And if I couldn't . . . problem solved. "Once you've committed to a plan to help her, pour everything you've got into it," Marty counseled. "After all that, if Kayla doesn't change her behavior, the bad will outweigh the good, and you'll need to let her go. But at least you'll know you made a strong effort toward helping her, and so will she."

Time to help Kayla kick this thing.

—

Marty and I used the rest of our time together to brainstorm ways I could help Kayla beat her tardiness. By the time I headed back to Gainesville, we'd come up with what I thought was a pretty good plan.

When I got to the office the next morning, I filled Abby

in first thing. I told her that for thirty days, Kayla would have to call me an hour before each of her shifts to report that she was awake and getting ready for work. If I didn't hear from her, I would call her to make sure she was up (or go to her apartment and drag her out of bed, if it came to that). According to my research, thirty days was plenty of time for Kayla to break her habit.

"After that, if she's late one more time this semester," I told Abby, "she's . . . she's . . ."

I knew I had to say it.

"She's fired." *Ugh.* It sounded so horribly final and violent. I hoped against hope it wouldn't come to that.

"Okay," Abby said quickly. *Whoa.* Had we really just agreed on something Kayla-related? I could feel the tide turning already.

As for the student at the heart of the conflict, she was on board too. For thirty days straight, I made sure Kayla was on time for every shift. She was my number one priority: I put her schedule on my own calendar so I knew when to expect a call from her. I had to wake her up a few times, but gosh darn it, we did it. She wasn't late to work a single day.

Then came the moment of truth: day 31. The first day Kayla was on her own.

I got to the office before she was due to arrive and positioned myself by the door, ready to celebrate when she walked in at ten A.M. on the dot. Then I waited.

And waited.

And *waited.*

Half an hour later, Kayla finally appeared.

As soon as I saw her pull into the parking lot, I ran into the bathroom and cried. I knew what I had to do when she walked in, but I just *couldn't*. So I didn't. I broke my deal with Abby, ignored Marty's advice to let Kayla go, and told her she could stay on the team.

I probably don't need to tell you how that went over with Abby. She lost trust in me—and rightfully so—because I had gone back on my word. At our next retreat, Abby and I had a big blowup. We had managed to bring our dark cloud with us all the way to sunny Miami. We made up—as we always did—but after that, Kayla became a taboo subject between us. Abby kept her comments to herself, while I continued to do what I could for Kayla with the dream that one day I could have an on-time Kayla *and* a happy Abby.

I went to the ends of the earth to figure out how to help Kayla be on time for work. I scheduled her for afternoon jobs instead of morning ones. I assisted her in creating her own self-improvement plan. I drew charts and graphs to show her how being late impacted our clients and her partners. I stayed up late searching the Internet for solutions. But nothing worked. And now, instead of being twenty or thirty minutes late, there were days she didn't show up at *all*.

I knew Kayla's actions were hurting the team—her constant lateness was already bad enough, but not showing up took things to a completely different level—so I made Kayla one final offer: Instead of assigning her to clients' homes and offices, I'd limit her work to cleaning only my own home and the Student Maid office. That way she could keep her job, but the impact of her chronic lateness (and now absences) would fall mostly on me. I'm sure Abby would have liked to see something much heavier fall on me, but it was at least a baby step.

One day, after Kayla cleaned my house, I came home to find a cup on the otherwise spotless kitchen counter. When I picked it up, I realized it was full of beer. Kayla was the only other person who'd been in my house that day.

The dots started to connect. Concerned, I called Kayla immediately and listened as she admitted that she had been struggling with alcohol and substance abuse for years. Recently it had been getting worse—hence the no-shows. How had I not seen this?

I knew in that moment I'd done all I could for Kayla. I couldn't go any further to help her; this was way over my head. I gently told Kayla she no longer had a job and urged her to reach out for professional help. She begged me not to hang up—I didn't want to—but I told her I had to. A few hours later, I got a text saying she was on her way to check herself into rehab.

I should have felt relieved that Kayla was getting the *real* help she needed, but instead I was overwhelmed with guilt and worry. I wondered if she would be okay without Student Maid and me in her life. I felt like I had abandoned her. I didn't even get to give her a hug good-bye.

But a few months later, something completely unexpected happened.

I got a call from the rehab center. Kayla was on the line for me.

"Hello? Kayla?" I answered anxiously.

"Hey, boss lady," she said cheerfully. (She always called me that.) "I wrote you a letter, and I want to read it to you before I mail it."

My heart quickly turned to mush. I understood it was a standard part of the recovery process, but it didn't make Kayla's letter any less meaningful. For the next ten minutes, she thanked me for caring so much about her, for believing in her—and lastly, for giving up on her.

Come again?

"I know it was hard for you to finally walk away from me," she said. "But I'm so thankful you did. I hit rock bottom, but now I'm taking control of my life again."

These days Kayla works full time—for a different company. When I run into her around town, she looks healthy and is quick to laugh. When I last saw her, she told me she had gotten a promotion and joked that it was probably because she's never late anymore.

Turns out losing her job at Student Maid was the best thing to ever happen to her.

—

Fear kept me from giving up on Kayla.

Not just fear of what it would do to her but fear of what it would say about me. If I kicked her off the team, wouldn't that mean I too had failed? Failed to help, after I'd made helping her and the rest of our students one of my biggest priorities? I couldn't face music like that. So I held on and held on and held on—and I failed anyway: I prevented

Kayla from getting the real help she needed, and I took about fifty steps backward in the relationship I had worked so hard to build with Abby.

I wish I could say that after Kayla left Student Maid, saying good-bye got easier. It didn't. And I wish I could say that Abby and I agreed on every good-bye in our company after that. We didn't.

The Kayla situation was extreme. But in general, when it came to making decisions about good people who just kept messing up, Abby *always* took the practical approach and drew a line in the sand. I *always* took the emotional one and drew a line . . . in the shape of a heart . . . with glitter glue. We were constantly at odds on issues like these.

It seemed like the only time we both agreed we should let someone go was when the "someone" was a Jennifer. If any member of our team intentionally acted in a way that violated our values, Abby and I both believed it was best for that person to leave Student Maid right away. (And luckily, Jennifer-like situations were rare.) I knew that we could never help an unethical person be ethical. They either were or weren't. But even the values, which were supposed to serve as a guide for these kinds of decisions, didn't help us see eye to eye. Take Kayla, for example: Abby thought her tardiness violated our "Don't leave us hangin'" value about teamwork, saying Kayla let her teammates down when she showed up halfway through a shift. But at the same time, I knew Kayla often volunteered to clean the filthiest room in the house so that her teammates didn't have to. Didn't that make her an example of the same value? Who was more right?

Because Abby and I could never agree on when it was time to give someone the boot, I had always made sure I was the one in charge of making the final decision, as I had been with Kayla. I'd empowered Abby to hire people, but this was a whole different ballgame. (Yes, yet another one of those things only I could do.) Our students depended on me for their livelihood. Their jobs helped pay for their food, rent, car payments, tuition, and other bills. Taking that paycheck away—especially from an extremely broke student—could profoundly impact their lives in a negative way. It could threaten their well-being and security. I felt that, as the head of the company, the weight of such a huge responsibility should fall to me, not Abby. After all, she depended on me for her livelihood too.

Handling every firing decision myself worked—until my speaking engagements picked up and I started spending more time outside of Gainesville than in it. By then, Abby had an entire leadership team by her side, and they were all in charge of running the day-to-day operations of the business together, which meant they had to handle disciplinary issues that arose with our students. Anytime there was a problem big enough to warrant a conversation about whether that person should remain with our company, the leadership team had to call me and explain the whole situation so I could decide what to do. The problem was that I wasn't available at the drop of a hat, and they'd often catch me when I was about to board a plane or walk onstage—

not ideal times to be deciding a person's fate. Some members of the leadership team were getting frustrated, saying they should be able to make these choices without me because they were more familiar with the students and the circumstances anyway, and Abby agreed. She called me one day to bring it to my attention.

"We need to be able to make these decisions without you," Abby said. "But no one knows how to make them because we don't have anything written down that we can reference. I think we need some rules and structure around here."

Rules? Structure? Not really my cup of tea.

We had a handbook (key word: "had"). Eva, the HR expert from the incubator, almost had a heart attack when I told her way back when that we didn't have one. (It's amazing my laissez-faire approach to HR didn't actually harm that poor woman. Eva, you're a saint.) So Lizzie, our first HR intern, helped me make one with Eva's help. It immediately became my least favorite book in the world. Its policies were, in my opinion, way too strict and unforgiving. So I just didn't follow it. I handled everything on a case-by-case basis instead (and I rarely documented any of it—please don't cry, Eva). I looked at each situation and did what I thought was most fair, given the circumstances. And because I didn't follow the handbook, that meant it was now useless: If I wasn't enforcing it, why should anyone else bother?

Although I didn't want to admit it, I knew Abby was right about needing rules and structure. As the company grew and our leadership team multiplied, I realized my case-by-case HR approach wasn't sustainable. Plus, if we'd had some rules, maybe the Kayla situation wouldn't have been quite so painful for any of us—Kayla included. It scared me to think about introducing rules that might lead to outcomes I thought were unfair, but I really didn't have a choice.

At our next workshop, I found our handbook in my office (at the bottom of a filing cabinet, coated in dust) and told the leadership team we'd go through each policy one by one. If we agreed with it, great. If we didn't, we'd talk about it as a team until we did. Hopefully, in the end, we'd walk away with a book everyone could follow that would treat our students fairly and help us determine when to keep hanging on and when to let someone go. And that would work even when I was onstage or forty thousand feet in the air.

Inspired by Kayla, we started with the three-strikes-you're-out rule on lateness.

"I don't have a problem with it," one person said quickly. "Seems fair."

"It's so *not* fair!" another shot back.

Clearly I didn't agree with this one either, seeing as how Kayla had kept her job well after the third time . . . and the thirty-first. So you know I had to give my two cents.

"I agree. It *is* unfair," I said. "How can we only allow students to be late *three times* over the course of *three*, sometimes *four* years?"

And that made Abby chime in. "We have to expect our

students to be on time," she said. "That's how the real world works."

"I'm late for meetings. You're late for meetings," I countered, staring down the people sitting at the table who had been late to *this* very meeting. "What if I told you that you could only be late to three meetings, and then you'd lose your job?"

Bring out the boxing gloves.

Everyone seemed to have a different opinion about what warranted a farewell. Some agreed with Abby and felt we needed black-and-white rules, while others agreed with me and preferred that we handle each situation as a one-off. Some believed a mix of both. And as it had been with Abby and me, compromise, let alone consensus, seemed impossible.

It took some time, but we finally arrived at a solution we could all agree on for tardiness: adding a fifteen-minute grace period to the policy. As long as students arrived at our office within that window, we decided, we wouldn't consider them late. I made everyone promise that we'd be on time too: If we were asking our students to be punctual, we each had to lead by example.

One down!

Except not really. After we said it aloud, something about it still felt wrong to me. I was suddenly back in the ring for more.

"What if they're more than fifteen minutes late but they have a legitimate reason?" I asked. "Like they locked their keys in their car?"

"Oh, here we go," Abby said. She'd heard me sing this song before.

After several minutes of, shall we say, *lively* discussion, we decided that students who were late for a legitimate reason or an honest mistake—like locking their keys in their car—would be excused. How could we punish someone for having a bad day? We concluded that it went against our promise to support our students. We also agreed that each student could have a total of five unexcused absences instead of three while they worked for us, and that after the fifth, they'd be asked to leave. In other words, there was more room to screw up than in your average company, but not too much.

Finally, we had a solution—for real this time.

That was just *one* policy, though, and it had taken a couple of hours to talk it through. You can imagine how long it took to get through the rest of them. But with time, we got through every policy.

We called the finished product the Guidebook: thirty-six pages of how to handle just about every kind of HR situation at Student Maid. I wanted to call it the Guidebook for a reason: It was supposed to be a book of *suggestions*, not a book of rules set in stone. I didn't like our first company handbook because it didn't have a heart or empathy. I never wanted anyone's destiny tied to an arbitrary rule. The only way I'd agree to get back on a plane and let our leadership team handle decisions like these was if they agreed none of the policies in the Guidebook would be absolute. They promised.

Still, something in my gut told me this whole "let's make rules" thing would backfire.

And by now you know that trusty gut of mine is always right.

—

About six months after the Guidebook went into effect, a leadership team member named Amanda told me about a conversation she'd had with one of our best cleaning-team members, Brian. Brian was sick, and it was our policy that he would need to bring us a doctor's note, or else missing his shift that day would count as an unexcused absence (and according to the Guidebook, after three of those, he would lose his job).

The problem was that Brian couldn't afford a trip to the doctor. So even though he was *seriously* ill, he planned to come to work because he was afraid of getting an unexcused absence. He cared about his job so much he didn't want to do anything to jeopardize it. He told Amanda, "The rules terrify me. If there's crackers or something at the office that I could eat, that might help my stomach."

My heart sank. Amanda's did too.

Amanda told me that many of our most engaged team members often expressed to her that the rules at Student Maid were scary. She said she felt like the leadership team was held to a different standard—that we wouldn't punish ourselves for some of the same things we disciplined our students for. No one at Student Maid had ever asked *her* for a doctor's note when she was sick, she said.

She was right.

I'd had a feeling this would happen when we put the Guidebook into practice. It hadn't actually become a *guide*, as I'd hoped it would. Some of the members of the leadership team stuck to the policies as they were written, no matter the circumstance. They appreciated the fact that the Guidebook laid out expectations clearly, with no room for ambiguity, and they believed it ensured fair treatment for all. But others, like Amanda (and me), thought that approach was too black-and-white. We wanted to treat the Guidebook like the guide it was intended to be and thought it was actually *unfair* to enforce the rules so strictly. When I'd visit the office between speaking trips, I'd notice the same disagreements Abby and I used to have starting to bubble up among the leadership team about the way certain disciplinary decisions were being handled.

So I brought it up at our next monthly workshop.

After the team got settled in our conference room, I opened the workshop by explaining what Amanda had shared with me about Brian. I told them it crushed me that a student had used the word "terrifying" to describe our rules. I never wanted anyone at Student Maid to feel afraid at work—for any reason. The nods I got in response told me they felt the same.

"How do you want our students to feel when they leave work each day?" I asked them. "How do *you* want to feel when you leave work?"

I uncapped my dry-erase marker and walked over to the whiteboard as they started calling out words and phrases.

"Accepted."

"Listened to."

"Significant."

"Supported."

"Empowered."

"Safe."

Within minutes, we'd practically filled the whole board.

"Now, look at these," I said, pointing to the results of our brainstorming session. "We know that we need to have rules and structure. That's important. But we also want our students to feel *these* things." I jabbed my marker at the words on the whiteboard. "So how can we have both?"

This next round of brainstorming wasn't nearly as productive as the first. We tossed around ideas, not really getting anywhere—until I remembered something from my poolside chat with Marty.

Marty had talked about how rules are black-and-white, but, as leaders, we needed to see shades of gray. In the example that he gave about Pete—whom Marty chose to keep in the company even after Pete falsified his expense reports—Marty didn't just consider Pete's actions. He looked at all the other details and circumstances surrounding the event. Pete was loyal. He was a good employee who believed in the company and who had always put his best foot forward. He'd also had a serious personal financial hardship that drove him to fudge the reports. Marty found it impossible to look at that situation from a black-and-white perspective because of those other factors. So he gave Pete another chance, on the condition that Pete never break the trust again. It was just as I had done with Kayla. I didn't see only that she was showing up late to work. I saw the hardships in her life that were driving her behavior, as well as her other positive qualities, which is why I gave her another chance. (And *way* too many more after that.) Abby had looked at the situation in black and white: Kayla could never be on time, which she was required to do as our team member, so she should no longer be on our team.

I explained Marty's example, and then I pulled his signature mentor move and hit my team with a scenario: I asked the team to think about how they would have handled it if Brian had actually missed work and shown up the next day without a doctor's note. The rules said that failure to produce a note—"proof" that he was sick—meant his absence would be considered unexcused. If team members racked up more than three of those, the Guidebook said they should be dismissed. But, I reminded them, Brian was one of our most loyal students and gave his best effort every day. We'd even had him hold down the fort at our office once or twice when we took our leadership team retreats.

After much discussion, the team decided that Brian, because he was such a wonderful team member, could miss work without a doctor's note without being penalized. The team said that because he had proven to be the kind of team member who wouldn't lie about being sick, they could take him at his word. We were getting somewhere.

Next I posed an even bigger question: How should we decide when we should bend the rules, as they'd just hypothetically done for Brian? How should we determine who would be given a second chance, as Marty had done for Pete? How would we know how many chances to give someone? And how would we know when we shouldn't give someone a chance at all?

(Okay, that was, like, four questions.)

If you think the discussion about that one tiny tardiness policy was lengthy, it's got nothing on the one that followed. It took several workshops to talk through these questions. I'll spare you the details, and instead I'll skip straight to the part where I stood in front of our students at a company-wide meeting and announced what we decided would be our new approach to rules and discipline at Student Maid.

(Drumroll, please. . . .)

"You see this right here?" I said to a roomful of our students, pointing to a long piece of gray duct tape on the floor. It ran from wall to wall, splitting our common area in two.

"This is called the Line. And here's the deal. We, your leadership team, are going to stand at this Line—figuratively— every day. We are going to support you, listen to you, care about you, trust you, empower you. We are going to give you all the tools you need to do your job. We are going to show up every day with the intention of investing in you and helping you become a better team member and a better leader."

I could tell by their faces that none of this was making sense to them yet, but they recognized that I was on my soapbox. There was no stopping me now.

"But," I continued, "we aren't going to be the only ones standing at the Line every day. We need you standing there too. We need you to try your very best every day when you come to work. We need you to make decisions with our values in mind. We need you to take the feedback we—and your teammates—give you, and we need you to take it to heart and grow from it. We need you to show up every day wanting to invest in yourself. Your actions need to show us that you believe in the company and that you care about our team. And if we see all that, we promise to let you screw up. We promise to give you the chance to improve when you mess up. That doesn't mean you get unlimited chances; it means that when you stumble, we will help you make an improvement plan. When you stand at the Line, we promise to be flexible with our policies, to accommodate you, and to be fiercely loyal to you like you are fiercely loyal to us."

I stopped to look around. They were with me. The duct tape was starting to make sense.

"And this relationship between us," I said, pointing to the leadership team behind me and then back at our students, "is only going to work if we—us *and* you—are all at the Line. We can't make you stand there. We can't help you if you aren't willing to help yourself. We can't make you care. We can't make you try. We can't control your actions. We can't keep making self-improvement plan after self-improvement plan for you. If we don't see you at the Line with us, we're going to ask you to leave."

We ended the meeting by asking everyone in the room—leadership team members, students, and me—to literally stand on the Line (and take a team selfie). It was just a piece of tape on our floor, but it symbolized so much. The Line is based on one overarching philosophy: If someone's good qualities outweigh the bad, we will fight for that person. That means that if someone's heart is in the right place, if they live the company's values, if they make decisions with the best intentions, if they put their best foot forward, and if they try hard, we will be fiercely loyal to them, and we will give them chances to screw up and learn. But if someone doesn't care about improving or if they don't overcome a weakness after we both commit to an improvement plan, then they have to go. At that point, their actions could become a threat to the culture, the business, or both, just as Kayla's did when I let her stay on the team after day 31. We can't just give people unlimited chances, especially when they are not holding up their end of the deal. If a student has to leave the company, at least we can sleep at night knowing that we gave them our all.

For the leadership team, the Line made it so much easier to know when to say good-bye without having to worry that they were making a choice that compromised our values, our culture, or our philosophy of learning by screwing up. But to make extra sure, I told them that no one should make judgments alone on how to handle disciplinary situations or rules. They'd still use our Guidebook—as a guide only—as they considered the circumstances surrounding the event. I told them they should also consult someone else on the leadership team to make sure their decisions were fair and balanced, and if two people couldn't agree, they needed to bring in a third person. I wanted to ensure that going forward, we led with compassion and humility, and that we made our people feel everything we listed on the whiteboard.

And just like that, the Line helped us take our policies from "terrifying" to totally in line with our culture. It helped us hold people accountable but also made sure that our people would feel cared for in the process.

Slowly, we were getting better at handling good-byes. Good thing, because we had some big ones coming.

—

From the moment we opened in Pensacola, trouble was written all over the wall.

The executive who'd reached out to me about bringing Student Maid to the area left her job right before our work started, and the remaining management team had a *major* stepmother complex for us poor Cinderellas. I'm not kidding. They'd ask for two people to come back to wipe a fingerprint off a mirror. They'd give out Rachel's and Sara's personal phone numbers to the guests, who would call at all hours, asking them to do things like "Please bring me a washcloth" and "Grab me a bottle opener" that weren't part of our service agreement. They'd call our students "kids" and talk down to them.

So when our contract was up for renewal, I whipped out my magic wand, turned my car into a pumpkin, and whisked the team away from that wicked, wicked place.

That good-bye was a no-brainer, thanks to all I had learned about protecting Student Maid's culture, even when money was on the line. But without the steady revenue generated by the condos, we'd need to make a big push for more clients. There was a problem, though: Rachel and Sara weren't salespeople. (They hold journalism and anthropology degrees, respectively, may I remind you.) They were both incredible with our students and knew how to make the Pensacola location *feel* just like Student Maid in Gainesville—which is why I trusted them so much with it—but they weren't exactly wheelers and dealers. When I hired them, their lack of sales expertise was the furthest thing from my mind. We had a major client lined up, so I didn't think we'd need to do any selling at all. But as soon as the clock struck midnight on the resort, I asked Rachel and Sara to put on their power suits and work on getting us some new clients.

They tried. The duo joined networking groups, reached out to friends and family for referrals, and direct-mailed potential customers, but their hearts weren't in it. It wasn't only that they weren't salespeople by nature; they just didn't *like* doing sales. It didn't fulfill them. Through networking and referrals, they had managed to build up a small roster of residential and commercial clients, but it wasn't anything close to cutting it.

There was never any real revenue growth. The branch was just maintaining. Abby did her best to help from afar with weekly meetings and strategy sessions, trying to help Rachel and Sara figure out ways to generate more revenue, but her efforts proved fruitless.

Abby was frustrated, and I didn't blame her. We knew

Pensacola had so much potential. We'd been there plenty of times before and found the market to be similar to Gainesville, so we were convinced it was possible for this branch to grow to a similar size. The real issue when it came to revenue was Rachel and Sara.

Abby suggested it was time to make a change. She thought we should hire a team more experienced with sales to take over in Pensacola. Not that she didn't love Rachel and Sara—she *so* did—she just expressed that she thought it was a bad move to keep them in their positions.

Just as in the Kayla days, I protested big time.

I argued that Rachel and Sara had dedicated blood, sweat, and tears to this venture and our company. No *way* was I giving up on them, especially when they hadn't given up on us while we worked with the beach resort. Hell would have to freeze over—twice—before I let go of two of the most resilient people on my team. Plus, giving up on them would be so unfair. I was the one who had put them in this position and pushed them to run our branch in the first place, even when they weren't convinced they could do it on their own. This was a new challenge for them, and it was outside both their comfort zones. I felt like I owed it to them to give them a chance to try a little longer. I was sure they would figure it out.

"A little longer," it turned out, was a year.

In that time the numbers didn't get any higher. But I didn't care about money; I cared about Rachel and Sara. So I continued to do nothing except cross my fingers that they would miraculously develop a love of and knack for selling that would save the branch—and their jobs. And Abby continued to be frustrated with my choices.

Toward the end of that year, Rachel came forward and made half my decision for me. She told us that in a few months, she planned to move to San Diego to be with her boyfriend, who was in the navy. Abby thought it was the perfect opportunity to take the salary we were paying Rachel and find a salesperson to replace her after she moved. But I had a different plan. I offered Rachel the opportunity to remain on our leadership team as our go-to writer in California (journalism major, remember?). Abby couldn't understand why we needed an in-house writer—and I'm sure you're wondering the same thing—but you know me: It's not over until, well, never. (Who could have predicted I would need Rachel's help writing this book?)

We couldn't afford to hire another person in Pensacola (especially because Student Maid had just gained a copywriter), so that left us with Sara heading up the branch solo. But that didn't last either.

About a year after Rachel left, Sara came forward and said she couldn't do it anymore. She saw the numbers and knew that Pensacola needed different leadership if we really wanted it to be a big success. Her heart was with our students and not in running the location. But she didn't want to "leave us hangin'," so she gave us six months to figure out what we wanted to do with the branch. After that, she'd move on to a job more in line with her interests.

I was sad to lose Sara, but with both Rachel and Sara out of the Pensacola equation, I could now focus on what we needed to do with the branch without having to worry about deciding whether to let them go. At our next workshop, we discussed it as a leadership team.

Surprisingly, in less than a half hour, we reached a unanimous decision: It was time to move on from Pensacola. We were focusing on so many other projects in Gainesville, not to mention my ever-increasing number of speaking engagements, and we just didn't have the resources available to make the branch a success.

We ended up selling the location. We were lucky to find a buyer who shared our values and our view on culture: a young entrepreneur who had a small cleaning company of his own. We sold the business to him for far less than we should have, but he graciously gave a job to every one of our students. It was more important to me that we leave them in caring hands than that we make money off the deal. It was a tough choice, but now that we'd made the decision, I felt relieved. Making it also helped ease the tension between Abby and me.

But there was one part that absolutely *sucked*: having to go to Pensacola and tell our students about the sale. I had no idea how much Student Maid had meant to them. As I stood in front of them and delivered the news, I watched some cry. I felt guilty. Horribly guilty. I knew this was my fault.

The whole way home I reflected on what had gone wrong. (It's a five-hour drive, so that's *lots* of reflecting.) How had we gotten here? What could I have done differently?

When it came to our students, I always made sure they

had the tools they needed to do their jobs. I asked our leadership team to pour their hearts into supporting them. I told them to meet with students to talk about their weaknesses and to make plans to help them overcome those weaknesses. I instructed them to set goals for the students and discuss with them what would happen if they didn't meet those goals. Why hadn't I practiced what I preached? I should have gone to Pensacola and personally given Rachel and Sara sales training. I should have helped them make a plan to hit their financial goals, especially when Abby was getting discouraged. I should have set a clear timeline for revenue improvement, and together, we should have discussed what would happen if the revenue didn't improve by a certain date. It wasn't Rachel's or Sara's fault that the revenue never grew—it was mine.

Up until that point, I'd only ever thought of the Line as it related to our students. But the Line had to apply to the leadership team too. Rachel and Sara had stood at it. Even though they weren't comfortable with sales, they gave it their best shot. But after hearing them report over and over that they hadn't met the revenue goals, I did nothing. The message I sent them by doing nothing was that I didn't care about making our Pensacola branch more successful. I wasn't giving it my all like they were, so they didn't feel supported in their positions and decided to walk away. I didn't do it on purpose—I was really, really busy—but that's the reality of it. I should have done better.

In creating the Line, I'd forgotten the most important piece: I had to stand at it too.

—

Did I lose on my investment in Pensacola? Yes. Did I lose on my investment in people? Never.

The time, money, and energy we invest is always worth it. Whether they stay with us for three years, three semesters, or three months. Even if we need to find them new jobs because we have to close down a location. It's worth it because we know what we've taught them will have a ripple effect in their lives.

Monique's experience with the key ring during move-out season and Lizzie's with payroll (way back in chapter 2, remember?) have had a profound impact on them both. I've received all sorts of letters and emails from students over the years with stories like theirs, which I keep in a shoe box in my office. There's a message from Danny, who graduated and opened his own health clinic in Louisiana. He wrote that the first thing he did when he started his business was identify a set of core values, and now the nurses who work for him say they prefer his clinic to other, better-paying ones because of the culture. And there's a letter from Katherine, who loved her job so much that she stayed with us from high school to grad school. She wrote that working at Student Maid taught her to be a leader and to believe in herself. Kayla's letter, of course, is right up near the top of the pile.

Over the years, my idea of success for people at Student Maid has evolved. And it continues to evolve. After The 45 walked out, I never wanted another student to leave the company. But now I celebrate their departures. I'm excited to see where their journeys will take them, even if that means they'll end up somewhere else.

But when it came to the leadership team, I still had trouble letting go. I saw them differently than I saw our students: They were my partners in growing the company. I didn't want to lose them. The situation in Pensacola with Rachel and Sara taught me that if I was serious about keeping people around, then it was critical for me to make sure that everyone's strengths aligned with their roles as closely as possible so that they could feel more fulfilled by their work.

Thanks to our focus on self-discovery and vulnerability in our workshops, other members of the leadership team soon felt comfortable enough to come forward and admit that they too wished their roles suited them better. What was interesting, though, was that when they'd share what they didn't like, someone else would pipe up and say, "I'll do that!" Which inspired a thought: Why should people have to do things they either weren't suited for (like Rachel and Sara with sales) or really hated doing when there were other people on the team who *were* good at those things and actually *enjoyed* doing them?

At one workshop, I asked everyone to write their own "job description." These descriptions were less about actual responsibilities and more about what they loved working on, what they needed in their environment to do their best work, and what things drained them or stressed them out. They worked together to swap the parts of their roles they didn't love with the parts of other people's jobs that they did. As long as the work got done at the end of the day, I didn't care how or who did it. We had enough talent on the team; why not let them decide who did what? For example, Maria, who oversaw HR, didn't like keeping up with the constantly changing HR laws and policies. But Bob *reveled* in researching and staying on top of things, so she volunteered to take over that aspect of Maria's job and report the findings to her. We couldn't take away every single thing people didn't like about their jobs, but eventually the team restructured their roles to the point where each person could leave work feeling fulfilled at the end of the day.

It was this discussion in particular that made it clear to a couple people on our team there was nothing Student Maid could offer that could make them feel fulfilled. They just weren't happy in their work. But that was okay. The whole point of this exercise was to find a way to make people happier, and if we couldn't make them happy at all, we encouraged them to move on with love and support. It was like the Line with our students—we knew we had given it our all and tried everything, which made it easier to say good-bye.

But anytime someone left—even if it was easier to part ways—it was hard to fill the gaps they left behind, both relationship-wise and workwise. So I started to think: What if I could find out if people had plans to leave Student Maid way in advance so that we could plan for it? We always encouraged the students to open up about their futures and be real with us about when they planned to move on. It was only fair that we do the same for one another.

At a workshop, I asked everyone to pick a date at least

three years down the road and describe what they thought their lives would look like then. What job did they have? What kind of impact were they having on the world? Where did they live? How much money were they making? Were they married? Did they have kids?

Then I told them it was perfectly okay if Student Maid wasn't anywhere in that picture. A few people looked up in surprise.

Some wrote in great detail and others wrote only a few sentences, but when everyone was finished, we went around the room and shared. At first it was a little uncomfortable. These were plans that would affect the entire team, and no one wanted to come across as selfish, but after some hesitation, each spoke up. One shared that she wanted to move to Portland to be closer to her family, and she hoped to be able to keep her position and work remotely after she moved. Another planned to move in a year to start a life somewhere else with her boyfriend. Another said confidently he was at Student Maid for the long haul. It was inspiring to see what everyone wanted for their lives and to be able to talk about our individual futures as a team. Now that I knew there were people who wanted to explore other options or work remotely one day, I had time to prepare for that. Talking about what we really wanted for our futures also made us promise to hold one another accountable to the dreams that were important to us, even if that meant moving on from Student Maid.

We'd finally gotten to this place where good-bye was a good thing for the students *and* the leadership team. It was all about making our time together count. And when that time came to an end, we vowed to wish everyone well and celebrate their send-offs, even if we'd miss them.

But my real test of this was yet to come.

—

I read the text from Abby again.

Hey, not sure what your schedule is like this weekend or tomorrow, I need to update you on something over video if possible. Let me know!

A message like that from Abby was unusual. She rarely needed to talk to me about Student Maid challenges. (We had come a long way since the shepherd's pie days.) And the fact that she wanted to talk over video told me something serious was going on, considering our rule about having important conversations face-to-face. Because I was away from Gainesville (as usual), video was the only option.

I couldn't wait another hour—let alone another day—to hear from her. So I texted back to see if she could talk right away.

Thirty minutes later, my phone chimed. Abby was Face-Timing me.

"Hey," I said, concerned. "What's going on?"

"This is really hard for me to say," she started, struggling to compose herself before she continued.

"I'm resigning from Student Maid. I have found a new opportunity."

I froze.

She was clearly waiting for a response, but my mind

went blank. I felt sick to my stomach, almost as I had when I'd first heard the news about Josh.

"This is just something I have to do for me," she continued. "I mean . . . I believe in Student Maid. I've given seven years of my life to this company. But I haven't been happy for a while, and you know that."

I did know that.

Abby and I hadn't been the partners we each needed for a long time. It wasn't just because we were constantly at odds over HR issues and Pensacola; as Student Maid had grown, we'd put our energy into different parts of the business. I focused on our big-picture growth, while Abby focused on the daily cleaning operations. We were on the same team, but at times it didn't feel that way.

In so many ways, our differences made us the perfect complement to each other. She wanted structure; I preferred to go with the flow. She pushed for hard lines; I pushed for guidelines. She focused on the present; I dreamed about the future. She was logical; I, emotional. At times in the past, those differences had both helped and hurt us, but now they seemed to push us apart. It became impossible for us to find common ground in our views on how best to manage the growing company, no matter how hard I tried. It had been affecting me, so I was sure it had to be affecting Abby.

We'd reached a point where it seemed like every conversation became an argument. The intensity blew the Kayla days out of the water because the stakes were always high. Abby and I never got handed the easy challenges. If it made its way to us, that usually meant the issue affected the well-being of the company and our people. Somehow we'd talk for hours and end up even further from where we'd started. I found myself cursing at her out of built-up frustration, and that wasn't the leader I wanted to be. *Ever.* I had built this company with relationships as the foundation, yet Abby's and my working relationship just wasn't in sync anymore.

I continued to try the best I could, and I knew she did too. Before our meetings together, I'd think through all the things I had on my agenda and practice how I'd present each one so that our dialogue could be more productive. When I didn't have time for our getaways because of my speaking schedule, I brought her along with me so we could still have our solo time. On holidays, I invited her to join my family if she wasn't planning on going home to be with hers. On her birthday, just a week before she resigned, I flew home just to surprise her for lunch. But it wasn't the same.

Abby was the one who had the courage to say it out loud. Really, I should have suggested it months ago. But see, when I said I now celebrated people's next career steps, I meant people. Not Abby. Abby isn't just people.

Losing Abby had always been my biggest fear. She wasn't just someone I worked with. She was deeply ingrained in the fabric of Student Maid. She knew everything about every client, invoice, and contract, everything. And she knew about *me.* She became not only my friend, but my confidante. What would I do without her?

As the conversation went on, Abby told me she was giving me a month to figure out a transition plan, and after that, she would start her new job, where she'd be helping another company grow. The position matched her strengths exactly, and I could hear in her voice that she was energized about it—something I hadn't heard in a while. We talked about all the things we needed to do for the transition, and when we hung up, I told myself everything would be fine.

But the next morning, I woke up angry.

How could she do this to me? I felt betrayed. Like someone was stabbing me in the back. (And amputating my right arm. And my left leg.)

Then I entered a state of denial. Was this really happening?

Then, acceptance. I accepted that it was her time to leave the nest and go after an opportunity that she was actually excited about. One that would give her joy instead of weighing her down. One that would ultimately be the best thing for the company too: If Abby and I weren't strong together, the company wouldn't be as strong as it could be either.

Abby meant a lot to me. Even though we both felt it was best to part ways, losing Abby felt a lot like losing Josh. With any significant loss comes grief. Unlike Josh, Abby is still here, but it didn't make saying good-bye to her any easier. It was one of the hardest things I've ever had to come to terms with in my life so far. But I found peace in knowing I gave Abby my all. I gave her more than I've given anyone, and she did the same for me. Student Maid would not be where it is without her. She kept me going on the many days I wanted to give up. And just like Josh, Abby will always be a part of me.

—

Invest anyway. That's what I've learned. I've found that even if you have the best culture in the world—where there are deep relationships, where people feel valued, where there's a high level of trust, where open communication and feedback are the norm—people will still want to leave. It doesn't mean something is wrong with your company or your leadership. In fact, I believe a leader's success isn't measured only by the people who are sticking around. It's also measured by the people who feel free to move on and leave even better for having worked with you.

I am thankful to every person who has walked through Student Maid's doors for investing in me and my company. No matter how long they stayed, no matter how eventful— or uneventful—their time was here, no matter whether they intended to or not, they have left their mark on us both. As we learn lessons side by side, some more painful than others, each person has helped make my company a better place.

Good-byes have been my hardest lesson yet. But as Josh's death taught me, some losses are out of my control. The only thing I can do as a leader is stand at the Line: I will give people my all, and I will do everything I can to make our time together count.

7 ~~NVILJ~~ COMING CLEAN

The heels of my pumps clacked down the hallway as I made my way to the green room. I opened the door and was suddenly face-to-face with a perfectly styled, perfectly airbrushed woman—who looked oddly familiar. I realized I was actually staring at a giant mirror. *Is that really me?*

When I'd first arrived, I had huge, dark circles under my eyes, the result of a night spent tossing and turning, wondering where our next big loan payment would come from. I had finally given up on sleep half an hour before my alarm was set to go off. Yet here I was, looking surprisingly well rested. Amazing what fifteen minutes in a professional makeup chair can do.

Nervously I checked the mirror to make sure there was nothing in my teeth.

I heard a tap on the door.

"Ms. Hadeed, are you ready?"

I looked at my sister, who was there for moral support. "You've got this," she said with a nod.

Man, I hope so. This is a big freakin' deal.

Five minutes later, a production assistant led me onto the

set to get me miked up before my first live interview on national television.

I was blinded for a moment as my eyes adjusted to the bright studio lights. Several cameras were pointed in my direction, and a small army of crew members fiddled with equipment I'd never seen before. The (very famous) news anchor shook my hand and wished me luck. Then a voice called out:

"We're on in three . . . two . . . one . . ."

Already?! I just sat down!

Breathe, Kristen.

Please don't screw up. Just this once.

"So let me get this straight, Kristen. You now have a cleaning empire, and it all started with a pair of jeans?" the anchor said.

Or at least I think that's what she said. The whole thing was a blur.

—

Let's be real: As much as I would love to say I landed this interview all on my own, I got it because a childhood friend—whom I hadn't heard from in years—worked for a major network and pitched my story as a feature to attract younger viewers. After looking into Student Maid, the producers wanted me to fly to New York to do a two-part segment about my business. Each one lasted all of five minutes. But five minutes, it turns out, was plenty.

To say that my phone blew up after each interview aired is an understatement. Friends posted pictures they took of me on their TVs with captions like "OMG!!" and "Can't believe it!" Family members called, telling me how impressed they were by my accomplishments. Student Maid alumni shared links to the videos, bragging that their boss from college was "famous."

It seemed like *everyone* I knew (and plenty of people I didn't) contacted me to say they'd watched and couldn't believe how far I'd come. "You must be so proud!" they said.

I was. I was *psyched*, actually. That a national news network thought my story was interesting enough to share with its millions of viewers was flattering, to say the least. It was definitely a pinch-me moment.

But the feeling didn't last.

Every time I ended up in the spotlight or Student Maid scored another accolade or media feature, the same thing happened.

Two million views on my TEDx talk? *Heck yeah!*

A feature in *Forbes*? *Whoa!*

Wait, *Inc.* knows who I am? *That's insane.*

I'd feel this rush of *I made it! We're amazing! Go Student Maid!* But then it was gone just as quickly as it came.

And now I know exactly why.

You see, the thing about that attention was that it focused only on "making it." The teaser for my TV news interview included footage of money falling from the sky before the cameras cut to me. They called my segment "From Rags to Riches." Anytime I gave an interview, it was the same: My story was prefaced with buzzy phrases like "One college student's fast track to success" and "How one

young entrepreneur created the perfect cleaning company."
Fast? Perfect? Yeah, right.

I'd read those headlines and hear those teasers and think, *They're making it sound like it was easy. Like I always knew what I was doing. Like I never messed up.*

But that was the message they shared because that was the message *I* shared. My speeches were about the lessons I learned, not how I learned them. My blog posts were full of advice for young entrepreneurs but said nothing about what it took for me to figure that stuff out. Everything out of my mouth was about what my company had done well. I talked about the fact that we'd employed hundreds of people, I praised our high retention rate, and I gushed about our "amazing" culture.

That rush of pride never lasted because I knew I was just telling the kind of story people expect to hear from an entrepreneur who's experienced some success. The neat, clean, uncomplicated, polished part. The side I thought everyone *wanted* to hear. The only side I wanted to talk about.

Until I started writing this book, that is.

My first go at it was more of the same—an inspiring tale about the wildly successful cleaning empire I had built against all odds and without so much as chipping a nail. I whipped up the first two chapters in a matter of days and silently laughed at everyone who had warned me it would be hard. It was a cakewalk.

But when I read back through what I'd written, I felt only a tiny ping of pride. My story was . . . empty. It had no substance. It was about a girl who wanted a pair of jeans and ended up starting a cleaning business that was now growing really fast.

A few weeks later, I was having dinner with an author friend of mine, and I asked him if what I was feeling about what I'd written—and how fast I'd written it—was normal.

He said, "Well, in my experience, you know you're writing the right book if it's really hard to write."

Those words stuck with me. I couldn't stop replaying them in my head. Was I writing the wrong book? I wondered. I thought through everything I had covered so far: our growth, our awards, our amazing students. And the more I thought about what I was writing, the more uneasy I felt. The manuscript was all sunshine and rainbows. I had breezed over early mistakes—the $1,000 on sushi, the trademark fiasco. I gave no hint at all about the screwups I was getting myself into *as I was writing*. I was losing sleep over Pensacola. Abby and I were drifting apart. Things at Student Maid were crazy. I wasn't going to include that stuff, though. Writing about that stuff would be way too . . . hard.

Oh.

I threw away everything I had written and started over. And over. And *over*. And almost threw my laptop off a balcony.

It's hard to talk about where you messed up. And it's even harder to know that once you send those words to the publisher, you can't take them back. (And that your mom and dad will forever have seared into their minds an image of you doing keg stands in front of the people who worked for you.)

But I *had* to get my screwups out there. I had to admit where I could have done better. I had to own up to my mistakes and be vulnerable. It was only when I did that I was absolutely certain I was writing the *right* book.

So I decided to try something. In my speeches and interviews, I started to share the stories I was writing in this new version of my book—the ones that didn't always paint me in the best light. And I found that talking about what *really* happened energized me in a way I'd never felt before. It made me feel alive. Talking about how I got through a screwup made me feel proud. Telling my whole story, warts and all, was liberating.

It made me wish I'd talked about this stuff sooner. That these were the stories I'd told from the beginning. I'd always been up-front with my team—why hadn't I shared my imperfect side with the public?

I don't know why I felt the pressure to seem flawless to the world. Maybe because I was young and thought I had to prove I was just as competent as seasoned CEOs. Maybe because I knew there were people who saw me as a role model, and I didn't want to let them down. Maybe because I'm a woman in business. Maybe because all those Friday nights in the bookstore, all I ever found on the shelves were stories about success. Maybe because as a society, we've made it really uncomfortable to talk about screwing up. Maybe because I've heard the phrase "fake it till you make it" about five thousand times. Maybe because, as a leader, I'm programmed to sell a vision of success because success, they say, makes people feel safe.

Maybe all of those.

What I realize now, though, is that when I talked only about what I got right, I wasn't doing myself—or anybody else—any favors. I want to be a role model, not an unattainable ideal. I want my story to inspire people, not make them feel like they haven't accomplished enough or can't measure up. I think about the people who sat in the audience of my speeches in the past, probably wondering why they were messing up when I seemingly never did. Why was it so easy for me to find success when it was so hard for them? I can't help but think—did I *un*inspire anyone? Did anyone decide they weren't cut out for owning a business or for being a leader because they were comparing themselves with the one-sided version of my story? I really, really hope not.

If I could go back to the times when I told those filtered stories of everything I did right, I'd talk about the things I speak about now. The things I wrote about in this book.

I'd talk about how I told people what to do instead of empowering them. I'd talk about how my poor decisions as a leader led to my shutting down a whole branch of my company. I'd confess that I learned the value of autonomy by being too controlling. I'd talk about the people I didn't ask to leave when I should have. And all the people I missed out on because I never hired them when I had the chance.

I'd talk about the times I hurt and let my people down. The times I didn't listen to them or make them feel valued. The times I failed them and they left.

I'd admit that there's no guide that explains exactly what it's like to lead and that no one gets it right the first time. You don't mess up a couple times and then skip your way to success. You mess up, get a little closer to achieving something, and then make another mistake that puts you ten steps back again. Sometimes you make the same mistake twice. Sometimes you feel like you want to give up. Sometimes you go to bed crying. These are the things I wish someone had told me when I was first starting out. They're things I wish more leaders would get comfortable acknowledging. Because let's face it, leadership is *really, really hard*. And I've learned that if it's not hard, chances are you're not doing it right.

Let me sing this from the rooftops: I am not infallible, and my company is not a utopia. In fact, sometimes we're both kind of a mess. Those dark circles under my eyes? They're pretty much permanent. At Student Maid, despite all we've learned and how far we've come, we *still* get it wrong. But we will never shy away from admitting that, because getting it wrong is what helps us get it right.

When The 45 walked out the clubhouse doors, I remember sitting there in shock. I was hurt. Confused. Humiliated. But then survival mode kicked in. I *had* to get those apartments cleaned, and fear of what would happen if I didn't was what made me call an emergency meeting and give my home address to sixty strangers who weren't too fond of me. I stood in front of them shaking. Unsure of what to say. Unsure of what to apologize for. Unsure of how to fix it. Who could've guessed that admitting I was unsure was all they needed me to do?

That night, I went from the put-together boss in the comfy armchair to the imperfect leader in her crammed living room. In the armchair I was distant, unapproachable, untrustworthy. But in the living room? Accessible, genuine, *human*.

And look what admitting I was imperfect led to.

I won my people back. And together we stumbled our way to building Student Maid. A place we protect and fight for. Where we learn to be confident and solve our own problems. Where we aren't afraid to confront difficult issues, speak up, or ask for help. Where we cheer one another on and recognize one another for our contributions. Where we feel cared for and supported, and where we can be ourselves. Where we learn how to be better leaders together.

I'm proud of what we stand for, and I'm thankful this is the business that chose me. I'm proud to lead it, and sometimes I get emotional when I think about how lucky I am to have the chance to be surrounded by people I care about so deeply. But I'm most proud of what it took to get here. All of the hard things, tough times, impossible situations, and collective mistakes that we learned from, and grew from, and that earned us the company we have today.

I don't know where the future will take me, but one thing I do know (for sure) is this: Wherever I go, I'll be screwing up left and right, and every step of the way, there will be people screwing up right along with me. As we go, we will continue to learn, grow, and build better companies together.

I wrote this book to show that behind every leader is a perfectly imperfect story.

So share yours. And when you do, you will give the people around you permission to screw up too.

ACKNOWLEDGMENTS

I can't believe it takes as many people to write a book as it does to clean a hundred apartments, but it does. To the village of people who helped me do it, this page is for you. And to anyone I left out, please forgive me. What can I say? Sometimes I screw up.

To my family

To my parents for being the kind who would never, in any universe, buy me $99 jeans; to my dad for giving me the tough love that shaped me; to my mom, my Bob, for being the person I've always been able to count on no matter what, for being my biggest fan, and for being my role model; to my sister for your creative input, all-nighter marathons, and for dropping everything and flying to me when things got a little crazy; to my Aunt Terry for reminding me who I am and for helping me find my voice; to my love, Spiros, for loving me even when I faced the frustrations of writer's block; and to everyone who had to listen to me say, "I can't. I have to write," in response to every question for two years: Your unwavering love and support mean the world.

ACKNOWLEDGMENTS

To my Student Maid family

To Rachel, my journalism-major-turned-book-editor, the most talented wordsmith I know and the only reason this is on shelves, what a dream it was to create this together—thanks for putting up with me in ways that no one will ever understand (and I probably shouldn't have in writing anywhere), we are totally doing this again one day (I know, I'm nuts); to Monique, the super (super) glue that held me and the team together throughout this journey, whose unwavering support and dedication kept us from falling apart—thanks for being my sounding board, my all-nighter companion, my alarm clock, my creative genius, and *my* head cheerleader; to Amanda, Maria, Tim, and Rachael, who never made me feel guilty when I had to focus on the book before our company and for handling things on their own, proving once again that they're capable of running the world; to our students, who are the reason I keep pushing to make our company better and who have taught me incredibly tough lessons throughout the years (even you, Courtney); to The 45, who gave me my first reality check and inspired my leadership obsession; to Lizzie, who made the $40K mistake and taught me to let people screw up more; to Kayla, who showed me that giving up on people can sometimes be the best thing for them; to Erin, for teaching me to listen more; to Abby, for standing by my side for seven years and for having the courage to call it quits in the end; to everyone who took a chance working with a little ol' cleaning company; to all our customers, who have given us chance after chance as we try to figure this business out.

To friends who became family

To Simon, for being one of my dearest friends and for going to the ends of the earth to support me and my dreams, for asking the hard questions and helping me realize I have a deeper story to tell, for keeping me humble, and for giving the best pep talks ever; to Josh, who was taken far too soon, who taught me to be vulnerable and to be present, and who I will carry with me forever in my heart; to Rich, my mentor, for selflessly giving time to young leaders like me, and for building a company that I look up to and model Student Maid after; to Marty, my mentor, for showing me how to balance how much I care about people with what's truly best for them, and for always picking up on the first ring; to my treasured friend Darlene for listening to me talk about the book for years and for reading every chapter (three times), and for not being afraid to tell me when they sucked; to Bob for welcoming me into your Barry-Wehmiller family and allowing me to share what you do with Student Maid; to Laurie, my hero, who I miraculously found and never want to let go of, my favorite voice to hear on the other end of the phone, who was there on day one and every moment after, even while kicking breast cancer's ass; to Jenn, who saved us more times than I can count, for being so smart and making me sound like I went to Harvard, and for keeping us on track when we were going off the rails; to Richard and the Inkwell team for being advocates for our ideas; to the Start With Why team, who taught me that together really is better, and I couldn't be more excited for the journey ahead; to Stephanie for being the most patient and encouraging editor in the entire universe, and for letting me extend my deadline "a few times" until it was the book I wanted to share; to the rest of the Penguin team for all the love and support, and for encouraging me to share the screwup version instead of the perfect one; and to Adrian for taking a chance on me and signing a book deal with a handshake, which only happens in a dream.

And to you, dear reader, for being willing to admit you don't have all the answers and for picking up this book.

RECOMMENDED READING

These are the books I read on those Friday nights in the bookstore.

Crucial Conversations: Tools for Talking When Stakes Are High by Kerry Patterson, Joseph Grenny, Ron McMillan, and Al Switzler

The Defining Decade: Why Your Twenties Matter—and How to Make the Most of Them Now by Meg Jay

Delivering Happiness: A Path to Profits, Passion, and Purpose by Tony Hsieh

Drive: The Surprising Truth About What Motivates Us by Daniel H. Pink

The Driving Force: Extraordinary Results with Ordinary People by Peter W. Schutz

The Five Dysfunctions of a Team: A Leadership Fable by Patrick Lencioni

Good to Great: Why Some Companies Make the Leap . . . and Others Don't by Jim Collins

How to Win Friends & Influence People by Dale Carnegie

Leaders Eat Last: Why Some Teams Pull Together and Others Don't by Simon Sinek

Man's Search for Meaning* by Viktor E. Frankl

Mess Management: Lessons from a Corporate Hit Man by Steve M. Cohen

The Power of Vulnerability: Teachings on Authenticity, Connection, and Courage by Brené Brown

Quiet: The Power of Introverts in a World That Can't Stop Talking by Susan Cain

The 7 Habits of Highly Effective People: Powerful Lessons in Personal Change by Stephen R. Covey

Start with Why: How Great Leaders Inspire Everyone to Take Action by Simon Sinek

Strengths Based Leadership: Great Leaders, Teams, and Why People Follow by Tom Rath and Barry Conchie

The Three Signs of a Miserable Job: A Fable for Managers (now published as *The Truth About Employee Engagement: A Fable About Addressing the Three Root Causes of Job Misery*) by Patrick Lencioni

Tribes: We Need You to Lead Us by Seth Godin

Wooden on Leadership: How to Create a Winning Organization by John Wooden and Steve Jamison

---

*Josh's favorite book

NOTES

Chapter One: The 45

20 **Millennials, born between 1982ish:** Fred Dews, "11 Facts About the Millennial Generation," *Brookings Now*, June 2, 2014, www.brookings.edu/blog/brookings-now/2014 /06/02/11-facts-about-the-millennial-generation/.

22 **It's no surprise to me:** Becky Mollenkamp, "Turnover," *CleanLink*, March 1, 2007, www.cleanlink.com/cp/article /Turnover—6327.

22 **The average company loses:** "Cleaning Industry Analysis 2017: Cost & Trends," FranchiseHelp.com, no date, www .franchisehelp.com/industry-reports/cleaning-industry-report/.

Chapter Three: Behind the Screens

81 **in a 2015 *Forbes* article:** Jeff Fromm, "Millennials in the Workplace: They Don't Need Trophies but They Want Reinforcement," *Forbes*, November 6, 2015, www.forbes.com/sites /jefffromm/2015/11/06/millennials-in-the-workplace-they -dont-need-trophies-but-they-want-reinforcement/.

81 **And a 2014 survey:** Jack Zenger and Joseph Folkman, "Do You Need to Lighten Up or Toughen Up?" *Harvard*

Business Review, March 10, 2014, https://hbr.org/2014/03
/do-you-need-to-lighten-up-or-toughen-up.

Chapter Five: Upside Down and Inside Out

158 **Four in ten of us:** Bank of America, "Trends in Consumer
Mobility Report," 2016, http://newsroom.bankofamerica.com
/files/press_kit/additional/2016_BAC_Trends_in_Consumer
_Mobility_Report.pdf.